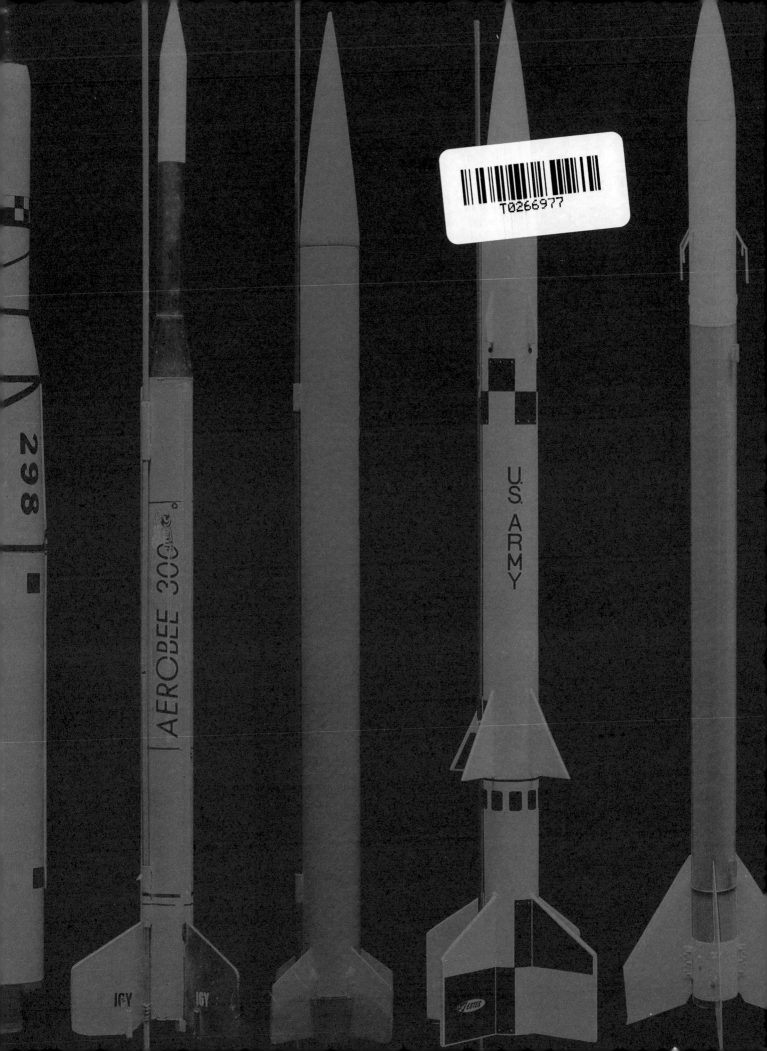

MODEL ROCKETRY

ALEXANDER PROCYK

MODEL ROCKETRY

AMERICA'S HOBBY IN THE COLD WAR

1960–1980

Other Schiffer books on related subjects

Rockets and Missiles of Vandenberg AFB: 1957–2017
Joseph T. Page | 978-0-7643-5679-7

The Rockets and Missiles of White Sands Proving Ground: 1945–1958
Gregory P. Kennedy | 978-0-7643-3251-7

Space Hardware: Artifacts, Equipment, and Sites from the American Space Program
John Gourley | 978-0-7643-6528-7

Designed by Christopher Bower
Cover design by Christopher Bower
Type set in Sofachrome/Univers LT 55

ISBN: 978-0-7643-6818-9
Printed in India

Published by Schiffer Publishing, Ltd.
4880 Lower Valley Road
Atglen, PA 19310
Phone: (610) 593-1777; Fax: (610) 593-2002
Email: Info@schifferbooks.com
Web: www.schifferbooks.com

For our complete selection of fine books on this and related subjects, please visit our website at www.schifferbooks.com. You may also write for a free catalog.

Schiffer Publishing's titles are available at special discounts for bulk purchases for sales promotions or premiums. Special editions, including personalized covers, corporate imprints, and excerpts, can be created in large quantities for special needs. For more information, contact the publisher.

We are always looking for people to write books on new and related subjects. If you have an idea for a book, please contact us at proposals@schifferbooks.com.

CONTENTS

PREFACE

Whom is this book for? When I started on this project, I thought the answer was obvious: for people who like rockets. Yet, as I thought more about it, I realized that I didn't really give rockets much thought since I last flew one decades ago, and yet I was now writing about them. What led me down this path, and who would want to follow?

My collecting passion is antique toys. One day I was scheming to open a toy museum, and it occurred to me that my cousin had a large model rocket collection that would make a great addition to the museum.

For background, model rockets come in three classes according to the National Association of Rocketry (NAS). Class 1 includes the rockets people most associate with model rocketry and are the focus of this book. This class uses no more than 125 grams of slow-burning propellant; is composed of paper, wood, or breakable plastic, with no substantial metal parts; and weighs no more than 1,500 grams, including propellant. (For the vintage of rockets described in this work, weight was limited to 453 grams, with no more than 112 grams of propellant.) Launches have prescribed guidelines, but they are easy to follow: keep to a suborbital trajectory, do not cross into territory of a foreign country without mutual country agreements in place, and do not create a hazard to persons, property, or other aircraft. There is also a requirement that the rocket must be unmanned, but at 1,500 grams, one couldn't even pogo-stick with one, let alone ride it into space.

Class 2 (High-Power Rockets) and Class 3 (Advanced High-Power Rockets) are beyond the scope of this book, but suffice it to say that they are big and impressive and require a heads-up to the FAA. Launch guidelines are strict and must be followed for the safety of everyone near and far.

Class 1 model rockets are not toys per se, but most are imaginatively designed with bright colors and outlandish themes to fire the model rocketeer's imagination. In this, their appeal is not unlike toys, which is what attracted me to them as a subject for a book. Since most are seen moving fast and at a distance, I thought it would be instructive to capture them in still life to appreciate the work that went into their design and construction.

While there are rocket enthusiasts who can boast a collection well into the hundreds, my cousin's relatively small collection is special. He began building rockets in the mid-1960s, when he was in junior high, and continued through his college years into the early 1970s with occasional additions thereafter. So, he stands in for thousands of mid-twentieth-century rocketeers, perfectly spanning the beginning of model rocketry as a fringe hobby to its explosion into the mainstream.

The collection, while not comprehensive, contains many classics and rarities of the period, specifically from industry titan Estes Industries LLC from 1963 to 1970. Just as important, my cousin was (and is) a master craftsman. He built them mostly as they were shown in the catalog, and to a high level. In short, the collection was built in period by a guy who knew what he was doing. These factors appealed to me as a collector of toys and midcentury ephemera, and as an enthusiast of the space race.

Many of the rockets shown here have the patina of age and use, and they unapologetically show it. While the first three rules of collecting factory-made products are condition, condition, and condition, model rockets, being kit built, are in a different category. Early kits are indeed collectible, as online auctions have consistently demonstrated, but they must be unassembled and in original, unopened packaging to fetch collector money. Assembled rockets, even well done, have a fraction of the value of mint-in-box kits, and one can argue on that basis that only unassembled mint-in-box (or bag, as the case may be) kits should be illustrated in this volume. But where is the fun in that? What would be shown is page after page of bare cardboard tubes and balsa. Conversely, one can argue that assembled rockets can be shown, but only if they are perfectly constructed and fresh out of the paint shop.

I do not make this argument. I feel there is value in capturing, not re-creating, the time when America was arguably at its peak; first in the world in science, in math, and on the moon. The rockets built in that period earned their bumps and bruises and should not hide under a veneer of new paint and graphics (though some rebuilds and re-creations have crept in where necessary).

Rockets from 1960 to 1980 are featured in this volume to neatly round out the first two decades of model rocketry, using Estes' first catalog as an admittedly arbitrary starting point (which contained only rocket engines). Listed rocket production years are from consumer catalogs; other production dates, which might be due to promotional campaigns, special offers, precatalog rollouts, postcatalog inventory dumps, etc., are not considered.

The subject of model rocketry is too large for any one volume. It can go many ways; a deep dive into technical aspects of engines and flight; a manual of model rocket theory, design, and construction; or a detailed history of the people and events that formed the hobby. Given my background and interests, I decided to go for a pop-art-style book as an introduction to the hobby, with context to the times and events that spawned it.

So, whom is this book for? It's for people who like rockets. But I also think it's for anyone who likes history, the space race, or mid-twentieth-century modern nostalgia. It's for people who fondly remember flying rockets with their friends, parents, or kids. It's for people who like craftsmanship and kinetic energy. I hope that it's also for inspiring people to go out and fly a rocket of their own.

As for me, while I may never have a museum, I realized I could at least have a beautifully illustrated reference book about early model rockets.

This is that book.

ACKNOWLEDGMENTS

I would like to thank Steve Lansdale at Heritage Auctions and Brian Anthony at Anthony Restorations for material on rockets in pop culture, and Sarah H. Jenkins at the NASA History Program Office and John Stone at Schiffer Publishing for help with chasing down historical photos of real rockets. Gregory P. Kennedy was a tremendous help in reviewing and supplementing the manuscript.

Sven Knudson was a tremendous source for model rocketry research and has assembled an excellent website of catalogs and other rocketry items at www.ninfinger.org/rockets/rockets.html.

I want to thank my wife for all her continuing support while I pursue all manners of distractions, earth bound or otherwise.

THE PHOTOGRAPHS

I wanted some drama to "fire the imagination," as some wise man put it, and thought that photographing the rockets against a black background to represent the inky blackness of space would give them some dramatic contrast.

However, many rockets have black fins, black nose cones, and other black bits, and these tend to disappear into the background. I knew this going in and just accepted it as suffering for the art. In general, they all look pretty good, except for the aptly named Black Widow, which just didn't work against black.

The SR-71 Blackbird, shown here, came out great even with a black background, but it was produced after 1980 and does not appear in this volume.

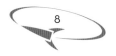

CHAPTER 1

ROCKETS IN THE MIDCENTURY

Morris Scott Dollens art from *A Dream of the Stars*, a proposed but never made film, ca. 1960s

TWO YEARS IN THE MAKING!

DESTINATION MOON

COLOR BY TECHNICOLOR

Produced by GEORGE PAL · Directed by IRVING PICHEL · Screenplay by RIP VAN RONKEL, ROBERT HEINLEIN and JAMES O'HANLON

Imaged by Heritage Auctions, HA.com

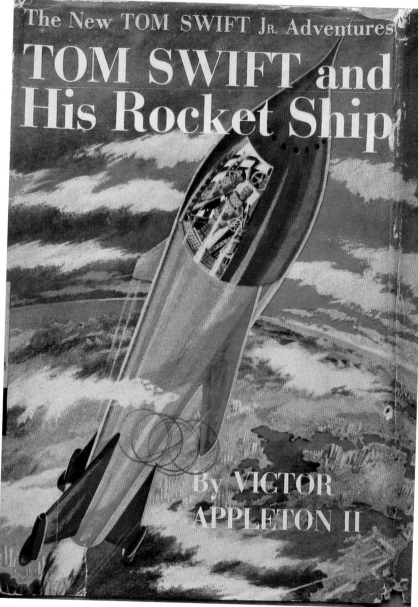

The New TOM SWIFT Jr. Adventures
TOM SWIFT and His Rocket Ship
By VICTOR APPLETON II

odel rocketry is one of the most popular hobbies of all time. Those who didn't fly them as kids most likely knew someone in the neighborhood who did. They can be found at any hobby shop and are on the shelves of big-chain arts-and-craft stores. They have been going strong for over sixty years after lifting off during the baby boomer years. That was not coincidental; they were the perfect product for the time.

Postwar America was obsessed with science and science fiction. The A-bomb, jet airplane, computer, and rockets were quantum leaps beyond Depression-era American experiences, and it fueled their imaginations. But Russia's challenge on these fronts—with outright supremacy in rocketry—fueled their paranoia.

Science fiction movies became the rage, occasionally celebrating space exploration for its own sake (e.g., *Destination Moon*), but more often exploiting paranoia of the outsider (*The Thing from Another World*), science (*The Fly*), and World War III (*The Day the World Ended*).

Isaac Asimov, Ray Bradbury, Robert Heinlein, Arthur C. Clarke, and other science fiction and fantasy writers too numerous to mention flourished in this period. Much was written before the war but was embraced by only a small, dedicated audience. As Asimov put it, "Dropping of the atom bomb in 1945 made science fiction respectable." And the race was on. Prewar carryovers such as *Astounding Science Fiction*, *Weird Tales*, *Amazing Stories*, and *Thrilling Wonder* were joined by new upstarts *Other Worlds*, *Galaxy Science Fiction*, and the *Magazine of Fantasy & Science Fiction*, to name a few. Together they pumped out science fiction in ever-increasing volumes.

While that was going on, the Air Force was doing its job to keep eyes in the sky. Chuck Yeager hit Mach 1 in 1947, and thereafter things only went faster and higher. Most of the 1950s was spent developing planes and missiles for ever-increasing payloads and range. But in 1957, Russia launched Sputnik into orbit, and, as Stephen King wrote in *Danse Macabre*, "Suddenly the Russians were looking pretty good in the old ICBM department themselves. After all, ICBMs were only big rockets, and the

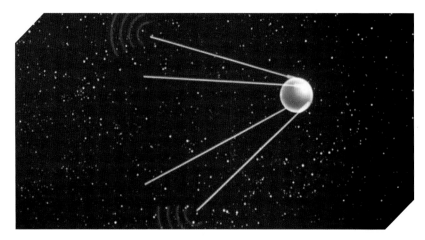

Sputnik, perhaps Russia's finest hour

Commies certainly hadn't lofted Sputnik I into orbit with a potato masher." King described how he learned of Sputnik in a movie theater. The manager stopped the show, came out on stage, and announced the news to stunned, frightened silence. Many didn't believe him.

Sputnik was seismic event, lighting a fire under Washington to speed up rocket development, both for military and civilian service, with passage of the National Defense Education Act and the National Aeronautics and Space Act (which established NASA). Five years later at Rice University, President John F. Kennedy famously declared that the US would go to the moon before the end of the decade.

What made the US civilian space program distinct from the Russian one was that everything would be covered extensively in the media, come what may. The Russians were interested only in promoting successes and burying failures (and they had some spectacular failures). The US approach invested the citizenry at the most fundamental level, sustaining long-term interest in the programs. It was reality TV, decades before such a thing existed. It was also risky, given the nascent US space program's habit of blowing up rockets on the pad or soon after liftoff.

The mighty N-1; not Russia's finest hour. It was meant to voyage to the moon, and it was awesome. It also made an awesome hole in the ground when it exploded. Three of its siblings went the same way before Russia gave up its hopes for a manned moon mission. Nobody made a model in period of this one.

It should be no surprise then that the mixture of popular science fiction, the Russian scare, and new aviation technology led to an epidemic of UFO sightings. UFOs were literally not on anybody's radar before the war; they simply were not part of the collective imagination. But the boomer years were primed for sightings. The Roswell incident in 1947 may have simply been a crashed weather balloon, but it started a UFO craze. It is no coincidence that *War of the Worlds*, published in 1897, did not become a feature film until 1953. The 1958 film title *Earth vs. the Flying Saucers* pretty much said it all. And the more said about Ed Wood's iconic 1959 *Plan 9 from Outer Space*, which combined flying saucers with zombies, the better. Flying saucers in that film were made from contemporaneous model kits, and Wood's special–effects artist (yes, there actually was one on set) struggled getting them because hobby shops in LA couldn't keep them in stock. For boomers, flying saucers were right up there with hot rods, monster movies, and rock and roll.

Toys of the 1950s captured the zeitgeist. Robots, space stations, moon explorers, space cars, and rockets appeared in abundance. Before the war, there were only a handful of space toys and robots. After the war, there were too many to count. A book that covered toy robots was simply titled *1,000 Robots*, and it did not exaggerate. Most were battery operated and imported from Japan in an invasion the likes of which General Tojo could only dream. Many were decidedly military, with ray guns and missiles liberally applied.

Imaged by Heritage Auctions, HA.com

Imaged by Heritage Auctions, HA.com

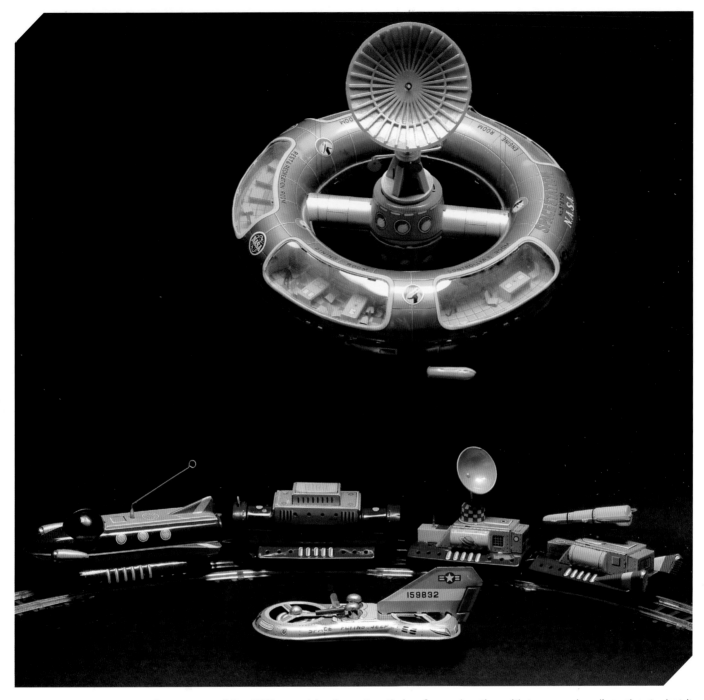

Space toys of the 1950s combined great optimism for exploration with tempered realism about what it would take to defend new territories from enemies, earth born or otherwise.

Judging by surviving examples, rockets were not as popular as other space toys. Toy robots and space vehicles performed much like a child imagined real ones would. Robots scampered across the floor, usually with blinking lights and clicking noises, and would change direction when bumped. Lunar rovers, space jeeps and atomic cars did likewise.

But what about the rockets?

Most were earth bound, having wheels along one side of the fuselage to roll across the floor in a decidedly un-rocket-like manner. A few sat on spring-loaded bases that hurled them into the air, but this was little more than an assisted throw. Although a child's imagination can do some heavy lifting, kids know a cheat when they see one.

This is the best of the tin toy rockets, and yet it is a poor example of rocketry because it can only wheel itself around on the floor.

Attaching a motor to the backside of a toy rocket changed everything. It now had to obey the same laws of physics as real rockets. Aerodynamics, balance, weight, and recovery all were necessary considerations for successful flight.[*] They were no longer *toy* rockets. They were *rockets*.

Model rocketry took off at the right time. The space race and America's emergence as a military, engineering, and scientific power after the war created intense interest among baby boomers toward science and engineering. These disciplines were challenging, exciting, and lucrative. They brought out the best and the brightest in the world's largest generation. These are the same types of people who later flocked to computers and internet technology, but back then, the projects they worked on were real, not virtual. Whether they were building bridges, dams, airplanes, weapons, or rockets, they could reach out and touch what they created. If something went wrong with a rocket, what potentially (or actually) got blown up was in the real world, not in a simulation. Model rockets—at least those powered with professionally built motors—were not prone to blowing up, but what happened after leaving the pad was always something of a gamble. The anticipation was often more exciting than the flight.

---

[*] Or not, as the case may be. My cousin, whose rockets appear in this volume, designed a glider early in his rocketry years. It was supposed to shoot up and glide down. He balanced it correctly for proper gliding, but not so much for vertical ascension. On its first flight it barely cleared the launch rod before turning horizontal, aiming straight at him, and chasing him across the field. My father doubled over with laughter; it was the funniest thing he ever saw in his life, before or since. Decades later he would still retell the story with a glint in his eye.

Electronic Countdown toy, ca. 1959. It was made by Ideal, but as a propaganda toy even the Pentagon couldn't do better. The little tykes would put a rocket on the carriage, drive it over to the launchpad, place it on the pad, and then set the desired flight height by cranking down an internal spring and plunger by an amount indicated in the flight window (Orbit, Moon, Mars, Jupiter, or Saturn). The rocket was launched by turning on the countdown dial, then hitting the fire lever when the counter reached zero. The rocket would take off, but not under its own power, which is the fundamental difference between a toy rocket and a self-propelled model rocket.

Model rockets were mostly imaginative creations, with great names such as "Mars Snooper" or "Snipe-Hunter," but real rockets and missiles were also well represented.

Before World War I, Germany's Kaiser Wilhelm reportedly insisted that German toy companies make toy submarines to familiarize boys with this then-new weapon of war, because they were going to be important to Germany's future.

The US government was not so overt in its approach, but PR departments at the Pentagon certainly made sure that the latest and greatest weapon systems were well publicized. Taxpayers needed to see tangible results for their money and feel secure that America could defend itself against all enemies (even if there was really only one).

Toy manufacturers got the message and responded with an endless supply of war toys. Again, many came from Japan, and there was a fantastic Japanese tin Midway-class aircraft carrier that was filled to the gunwales with irony. Model rocket companies followed suit, and scale models of missiles such as Honest John and WAC Corporal were soon flying around the country. And when NASA stepped in, turning the Titan missile into the Gemini-Titan rocket, models of those were soon firing off, as were, of course, the Saturn rockets.

Model rockets built off the successes of the 1960s and exploded, so to speak, during the 1970s. Comparison of the 1971 Estes catalog with the 1970 catalog shows a quantum leap in style and polish. Rockets made the transition from boomers to Gen Xers, and from there it was ever onward and upward. They seemed almost a rite of passage—either you flew them with your dad, flew them yourself, or flew them with your son; sometimes all three, at once or sequentially.

All this was actively supported by rocketry clubs—almost every high school had one. Newsletters, magazines, and the National Association of Rocketry (NAR) did their part to fan the flames. School support for clubs may have waned since the 1970s, but the internet has more than stepped in to keep interest strong.

Rocket plans, tips, tricks, and new technology all are actively discussed. While many still fly rockets that are little different from their Cold War predecessors, the popularity of high-powered rockets, which require FAA approval, is on the rise.

And it doesn't stop there. While the large Class 1 Saturn V rocket from Estes stands about 40 inches tall, a video of a guy launching his *36-foot* Saturn V replica can be found online. One hopes he did not store the propellant in his garage, because a mishap would have taken out his entire block. Similarly, the British TV show *Top Gear* made a space shuttle out of a three-wheel Reliant Robin car, largely on the preposterous basis that it looked a bit like the real space shuttle, and attached it to a 30-foot booster.

There was a mishap. It went up fine, but separation was not to be had, and it planted itself into the ground—thankfully at a missile test site—with an almighty explosion.

The point is, model rocketry is still with us, and it is still exciting.

CHAPTER 2

MODEL ROCKET PROPULSION

CARBON DIOXIDE ENGINES

ALPHA-1 1965-68

Patent 2,918,751, assigned to Robert J. Johnson, Scientific Products Company, Richmond, Virginia, on November 14, 1957

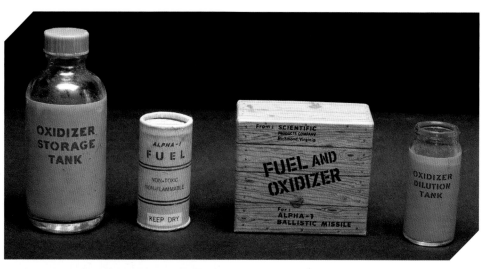

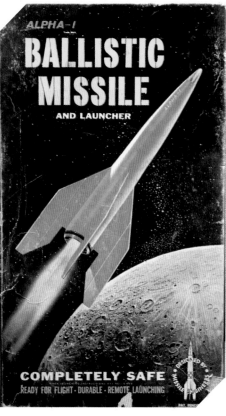

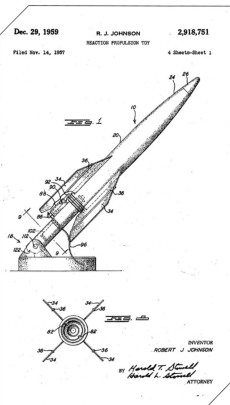

Alpha–1 was from Scientific Products Company of Richmond, Virginia, but was originally produced by Texaco Experiment Inc.

The rocket was powered by pressurized carbon dioxide generated from a sodium carbonate–citric acid reaction, though they simply referred to them as "oxidizer" and "fuel," never revealing the real chemicals, which was somewhat condescending for a toy that was supposed to be educational. It appears with various packaging, called either "Alpha–1 Ballistic Missile" or "Apollo Alpha–1," clearly glomming on to the Apollo space program. Either one can be found with box art claiming that it was "designed by missile engineers, tested at Cape Kennedy," which seems a bit dubious. Lunar–I was a two–stage version of Alpha–1.

Although they flew like pyrotechnic rockets, they didn't fly far, and the lack of fiery combustion, combined with the insistence that they are "completely safe" (though they reportedly came down like lawn darts), relegates them to the junior varsity of model rocketry.

SOLID-FUEL ENGINES

Model rockets are powered by solid–fuel engines, which burn propellant. The model rocket engine is at the heart of the model rocket system and is a major contributor to the hobby's safety record. Hobbyists do not have to handle or mix their own propellants— that job is done by professionals. Most model rocket engines have a cardboard casing, a clay nozzle, a propellant charge, a delay element, and an ejection charge to activate the recovery system.

The nomenclature on an engine comprises three parts that describe its power and characteristics. Typical engines codes are A8–3, B6–4, and C6–5. The power of the engine is referenced in a letter designation (1/4A, 1/2A, A, B, or C). Engines are categorized by total impulse, which is the product of the average thrust times the thrust duration. In the early 1960s, total impulse was expressed in pound-seconds; since 1967, when the model rocket industry adopted the metric system, total impulse has been expressed in newton-seconds (4.45 newtons = 1 pound). Each succeeding letter has twice the power of the previous letter.

Lunar–I
1965–68

A number after the letter (e.g., A8, B4, C6) shows the engine's average thrust in newtons. It is possible to have different combinations of average thrust and duration to produce the same total impulse. For example, Estes produces B4 and B6 engines. Both have a total impulse of 5 newton-seconds, but the B4 has a thrust duration of 1.1 seconds while the B6 produces thrust for only 0.8 seconds. While both deliver the same overall power, the B6 can launch a slightly heavier rocket than a B4, though obviously not as far.

The third component of the engine nomenclature is a whole number that expresses the duration of the time delay in seconds. When the engine exhausts its propellant, the rocket can be traveling at a high rate of speed, and deploying a recovery system at that time would likely shred the parachute. Therefore, the engine contains a delay element that produces smoke but no thrust to allow the rocket to slow down through a combination of aerodynamic drag and gravity.

Once the rocket has burned through the delay element, an ejection charge fires through the top of the engine casing to deploy the recovery system.

Initially, Estes produced engines in casings that measured 18 mm in diameter by 70 mm long. These were suitable for total impulse ranges of 1/4A, 1/2A, A, B, and C. The earliest model rocket engines used pounds to express thrust; hence the engine coding was along the lines of B.8-4. The .8 is the average thrust in pounds.

In 1968, model rocket engines underwent several major changes. As mentioned above, total impulse was now expressed in newton-seconds, and ranges were redefined. The clay nozzles were redesigned to provide greater efficiency, and the cardboard casings became thinner. These changes allowed Estes to expand its engine offerings into the C power range.

In 1970, Estes introduced "D" engines for larger model rockets and high-performance flight. D engines are bigger in diameter (24 mm) than standard engines and have twice the total impulse power of the C engine.

In the smaller impulse ranges (1/4A, 1/2A, and A), the propellant and time delay rarely exceeded half the length of the engine casing. Therefore, Estes offered "short" engines that were the same diameter (18 mm) as their "standard" engines but in shorter casings (44 mm long). Designations for these engines contained an "S" suffix—1/4A6-2S, 1/2A-2S, and A5-2S being examples.

In 1972, Estes replaced these engines with their "Mini Engines" for their "Mini Brute" range of rockets. These engines were smaller in diameter and length (13 mm × 40 mm, respectively) than standard engines. They had a "T" at the end of the designation (e.g., 1/2A3-4T) and were often referred to as T engines. Small-diameter rockets were made that could use only these engines. After a couple of years, Mini Engines replaced short engines altogether.

Other companies, such as Flight Systems and Coaster, introduced larger motors in D, E, and F classes throughout the 1960s. These were charged with black powder, but Rocket Development Corp. (RDC) developed high-powered engines with a composite propellant similar to that found in real missiles. These engines and the large-scale rockets they powered were never as popular as smaller rockets powered by 1/4A-D series engines, but high-powered rocketry has undergone a renaissance and is now avidly practiced.

The lower-stage engines of multistage rockets do not have ejection charges. Instead, they fire sparks upward to ignite upper-stage engines. Their delay designation is therefore 0 (e.g., A8-0).

The motor manufacturers published detailed charts for all engines that list total impulse, maximum liftoff weight, maximum thrust, thrust duration, and time delay—essentially everything the rocketeer needed to know to predict the performance of his or her rocket.

The rockets illustrated in this book are powered by A, B, or C engines and are recovered with parachutes, unless otherwise stated in the caption.

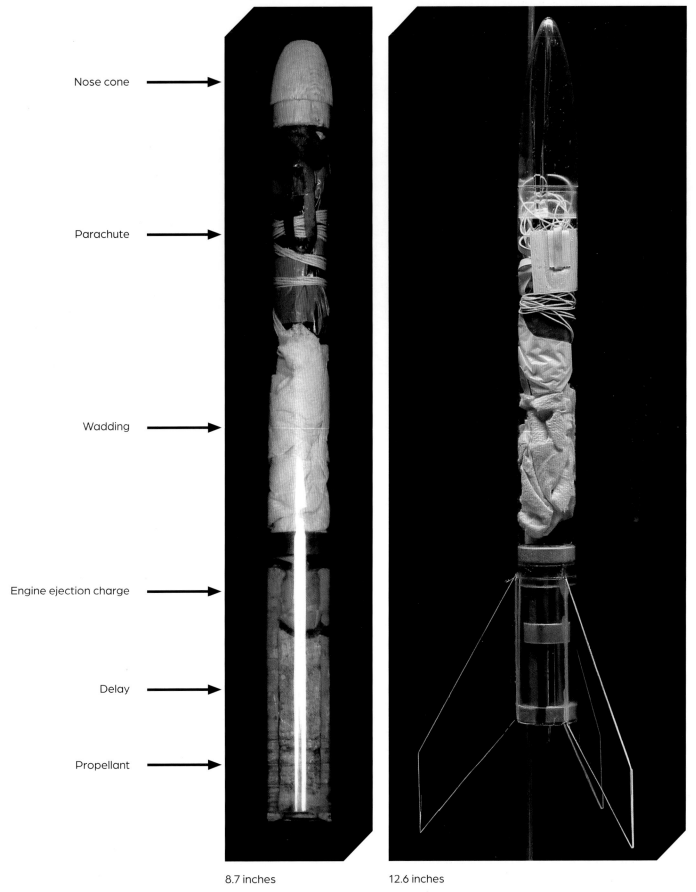

Nose cone

Parachute

Wadding

Engine ejection charge

Delay

Propellant

8.7 inches

12.6 inches

Estes Phantom (1963–96) is a single-stage rocket in appearance but is clearly an educational aid and not a working rocket. Phantom first acquired fins and a plastic nose cone in 1973. Centuri cataloged a similar rocket called Visible Astro in 1971.

COLD-POWERED ROCKETS

Vashon Industries were pioneers in cold-powered rockets, based out of Vashon Island, Washington. Vashon introduced the rockets in the 1960s and was bought out by Damon in 1971. Their rockets became the foundation of the Estes Cold Power line.

Their main advantage was that you could launch them anywhere, without restriction, and they were safe. Certain areas of the country had age restrictions for purchasing conventional pyrotechnic motors, and some areas banned them as a fire hazard. They can still be flown, using ozone-friendly RP134 refrigerant as a propellant.

Cold-powered rockets were somewhat sophisticated. They were powered by compressed gas, which in those pre-ozone-depletion days was Freon-12. The engine was an aluminum tank, charged with gas through a fill valve. A retaining pin held a plug in in the nozzle while filling was ongoing. To launch, the retaining pin was pulled. An alternative remote-launching mechanism used fusible wire from a regular igniter. When hit with electricity, it would melt and release the nozzle plug.

Because there was no ejection charge, an ingenious but infuriating mechanism was used for separation and parachute release. The rocket was split into two largely equal pieces. A springy disk was on top of the motor section, inside an expandable cylinder and in pressure communication with the engine. The top part of the rocket slipped over this assembly, and when the motor was filled, pressure pushed on the disk, which in turn pushed on the sides of the cylinder, expanding it to hold the top part of the rocket tight. After the fuel was exhausted, the disk retracted, releasing the top, which, because of its weight, fell off and released the parachute. There were paper disks between the engine and spring assembly to slow pressure leak-off and to delay release.

1973 catalog showing cold-powered rocket design

The mechanism was infuriating because, until you pressurized the engine at the pad, the top part was never held onto the bottom, so it would fall off whenever you handled the rocket. Such as, for example, when returning it to a table after photographing it, where the top could fall off, roll off the table, and drag the rest of the rocket with it to the floor. Hypothetically.

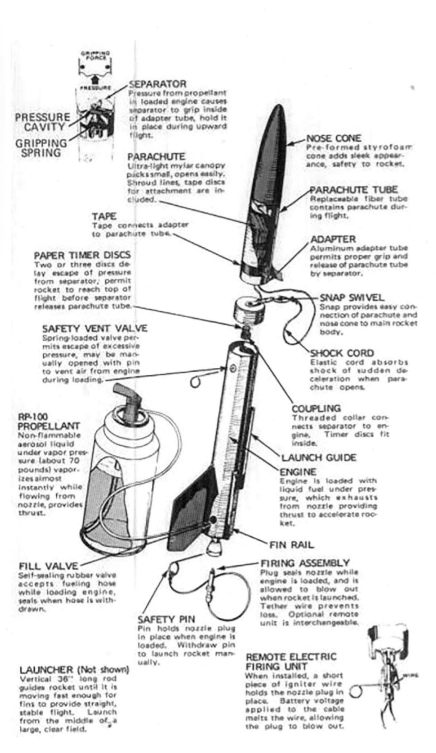

SEPARATOR
Pressure from propellant in loaded engine causes separator to grip inside of adapter tube, hold it in place during upward flight.

PRESSURE CAVITY

GRIPPING SPRING

PARACHUTE
Ultra-light mylar canopy packs small, opens easily. Shroud lines, tape discs for attachment are included.

TAPE
Tape connects adapter to parachute tube.

PAPER TIMER DISCS
Two or three discs delay escape of pressure from separator; permit rocket to reach top of flight before separator releases parachute tube.

SAFETY VENT VALVE
Spring-loaded valve permits escape of excessive pressure, may be manually opened with pin to vent air from engine during loading.

RP-100 PROPELLANT
Non-flammable aerosol liquid under vapor pressure (about 70 pounds) vaporizes almost instantly while flowing from nozzle, provides thrust.

FILL VALVE
Self-sealing rubber valve accepts fueling hose while loading engine, seals when hose is withdrawn.

LAUNCHER (Not shown)
Vertical 36" long rod guides rocket until it is moving fast enough for fins to provide straight, stable flight. Launch from the middle of a large, clear field.

NOSE CONE
Pre-formed styrofoam cone adds sleek appearance, safety to rocket.

PARACHUTE TUBE
Replaceable fiber tube contains parachute during flight.

ADAPTER
Aluminum adapter tube permits proper grip and release of parachute tube by separator.

SNAP SWIVEL
Snap provides easy connection of parachute and nose cone to main rocket body.

SHOCK CORD
Elastic cord absorbs shock of sudden deceleration when parachute opens.

COUPLING
Threaded collar connects separator to engine. Timer discs fit inside.

LAUNCH GUIDE

ENGINE
Engine is loaded with liquid fuel under pressure, which exhausts from nozzle providing thrust to accelerate rocket.

FIN RAIL

FIRING ASSEMBLY
Plug seals nozzle while engine is loaded, and is allowed to blow out when rocket is launched. Tether wire prevents loss. Optional remote unit is interchangeable.

SAFETY PIN
Pin holds nozzle plug in place when engine is loaded. Withdraw pin to launch rocket manually.

REMOTE ELECTRIC FIRING UNIT
When installed, a short piece of igniter wire holds the nozzle plug in place. Battery voltage applied to the cable melts the wire, allowing the plug to blow out.

ESTES

"Imagine the thrill of pressing the firing switch and watching a rocket you have built roar skyward in a cloud of smoke, leaving a vapor trail behind as it shrinks into just a speck."

These are the first words in Estes' 1962 catalog, printed five years after Vern Estes began his career in model rocketry by supplying engines to Model Missiles, Inc., a Denver company founded in 1957 by G. Harry Stine and Orville Carlisle. Carlisle, a Nebraska shoe store owner and amateur pyrotechnist, teamed up with Stine to develop a model rocket powered by prepackaged solid-propellant engines. This eliminated home-mixing of propellants, which were injuring—if not killing—rocketry hobbyists at an alarming rate.

Carlisle developed the ancestor of modern model rocket engines for his brother, who gave demonstrations of model aircraft to area schools. Orville's brother wanted something "space age" to finish his miniature air shows. Stine, who had been an engineer at White Sands Proving Ground in New Mexico, was a frequent contributor to magazines such as *Popular Science*. He wrote a column urging aspiring rocket builders to seek professional guidance before engaging in their research. Carlisle saw the column and contacted Stine about his invention. Seeing the potential, Stine and Carlisle quickly teamed up to form Model Missiles, Inc., the world's first model rocket company.

Carlisle and Stine turned to the Estes family for ideas about how to manufacture safe engines, because they owned a fireworks business. The elder Estes recommended their son Vern Estes, who was a building contractor at the time. In 1958, Vern went into the engine business with a machine of his own design called "Mabel," and began to produce engines at the rate of ten per minute. This was in excess of Model Missiles' needs, and Vern sold the excess through magazine ads.

Model Missiles soon went out of business, and in 1960 Estes published their first catalog containing rocket motors and rocket plans and parts and never looked back. In 1961, the Estes plant was relocated for safety concerns to a 77-acre tract of land on the outskirts of Penrose, Colorado.

Estes' early catalogs appealed to Cold War angst and the excitement of space exploration by stating that

the type of youth science study provided by model rocketry is necessary if this country is to survive the coming years of the cold war and, if it should arise, a major war. Practical experience, gained from working with the same principles, theories, and ideas which will be used in his profession, is necessary if today's youth are to be motivated to study for vital careers in the space sciences. As such, they become pioneers, pioneers of the greatest frontier man has ever faced.

Estes spared nothing to provide the rocketeer everything he or she needed to fully assemble, understand, fly, and evaluate their rockets. Materials, tools, rocket components, and graphics all were available. Assembly and painting tips were liberally offered. Detailed engine specifications were published. Altiscopes with associated computing equipment were available to track rockets in flight, to determine how closely theoretical calculations came to actual altitudes reached. This was true model rocketry, not just building small models of rockets but also modeling the tools and techniques of their full-sized brethren.

Estes also published a magazine, *Model Rocket News*, for "useful tips 'n hints, rocket plans, technical reports, and interesting and enjoyable reading," to quote the catalog. A selection of rockets built from plans in MRN are shown in chapter 6. Occasionally these plans would later appear as rocket kits in the catalog.

Many early rockets were identified as part of an Astron range. This appellation was not applied to the scale-model-series rockets. Starting in 1966, occasional newcomers such as Big Bertha and Mars Snooper were not in the Astron range, until they were, or not, as the case may be. For example, Big Bertha was brought into the Astron family in 1971, but Mars Snooper never was. There was no explanation for any of this in the catalogs; the name appeared to be a marketing device known only to Estes.

Vern Estes sold the business in 1969 to Damon Corp., a NYSE-listed medical products manufacturer based in Needham Heights, Massachusetts. He remained on as a consultant. Damon expanded the Penrose facility and bought rival Centuri in 1970, though Centuri was listed as the parent company because it was based in more tax-advantaged Arizona.

SINGLE-STAGE ROCKETS

The original Birdie used Estes Short engines. It was redesigned for Mini Engines and first appeared in the 1972 catalog.

All the rockets on this page had "featherweight recovery," which meant they just fell back to Earth after ejecting their motor.

BIRDIE
1971-73

A kit was offered in 1969–70 to convert your own birdie. Later kits came with a birdie. 2.8 inches.

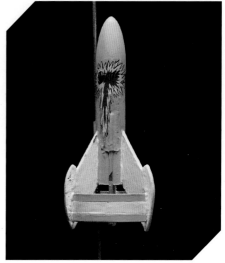

SPRITE
1966-73

Tumble recovery. 5.3 inches.

MOSQUITO
1972-2002

3.9-inch Mini Engine

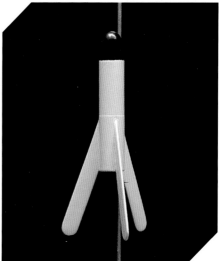

STREAK
1963-87

Streak contained two fin configurations in the instructions. These are the competition fins, which were not shown in the catalog illustrations. 5.6 inches.

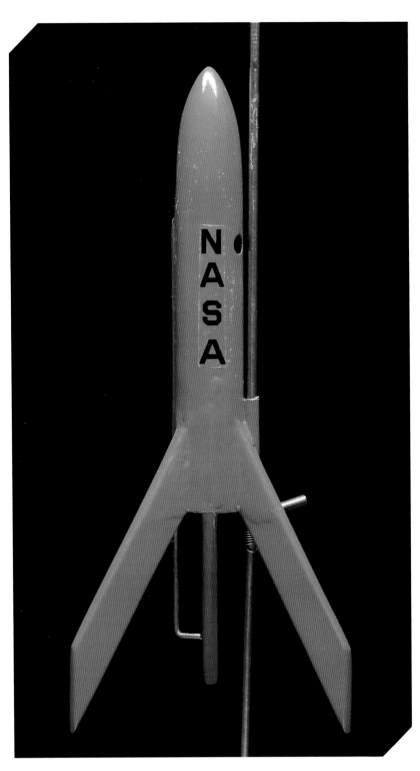

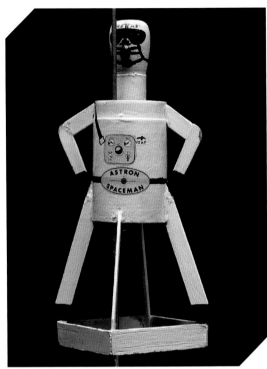

SPACEMAN
1964-71

The face illustration in the 1964 catalog was just goofy. Later catalog designs were better. The instructions had several alternative ideas, and my cousin thankfully went with the fighter pilot option. Recovery was by landing on his head.

7.25 inches

1964 catalog illustration

1970 catalog illustration

SCOUT
1961-85

Scout was Estes first rocket kit and was unique in that it had a tumble recovery system. The motor would eject and get caught by the metal clip hanging below the fuselage, unbalancing the rocket and causing it to tumble. This built up air resistance to gently drop it to the ground. It didn't need it; it was built like a tank. Scout became Scout II in 1986. It was the same rocket, just easier to build with precut fins. Tumble recovery. 7.0 inches.

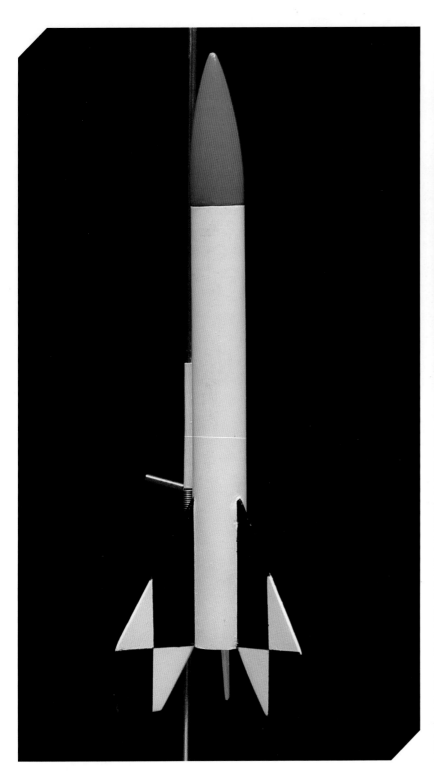

ASTRON MARK
1963-71

The Astron used a unique body tube. Most tubes were spiral wound; the Astron Mark used a body tube that was parallel wound and was slightly fatter. Vern Estes's wife, Gleda, hand-wound the original parallel wound tubes. In 1972, the Astron Mark became the Mark II, with the easier-to-produce spiral-wound body tube and midbody separation. The redesigned Mark II remained in production until the mid-1980s and last appeared in the 1984 catalog. 9.12 inches.

MINI-BERTHA
1972-82

Mini Engine. 11.25 inches.

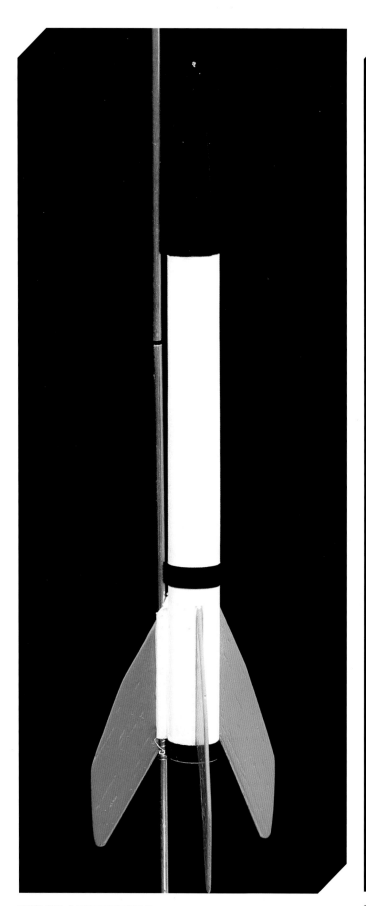

SKY HOOK
1964–88
12 inches

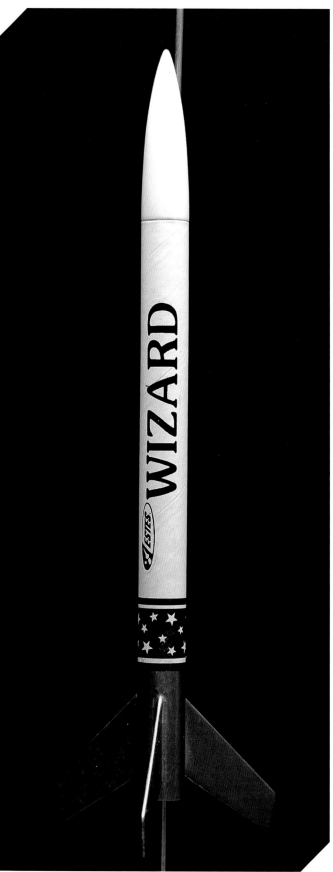

WIZARD
1980-92
12 inches

MARS LANDER
1969-83

Mars Lander was a skill level 4 rocket until 1973, when it was upgraded to skill level 5, the top level. They meant it. The body is fabricated by wrapping and joining multiple sheets around a core, and each leg is built from multiple components, hinged at the core, and damped with a rubber band shock absorber. It probably never should have been skill level 4, but perhaps the bump-up in skill level reflected a demise in modeling skill, or patience, among the general populace.

Unfortunately, rubber bands were a poor choice of material since they degraded over time. The rubber bands in this example were replaced by cutting an access hatch. The hatch was expertly replaced and is now undetectable.

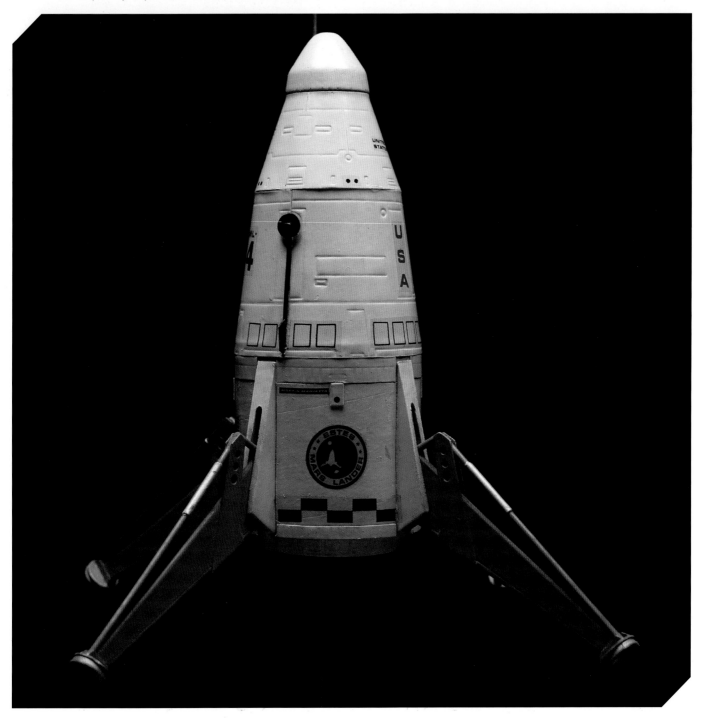

12 inches

Estes

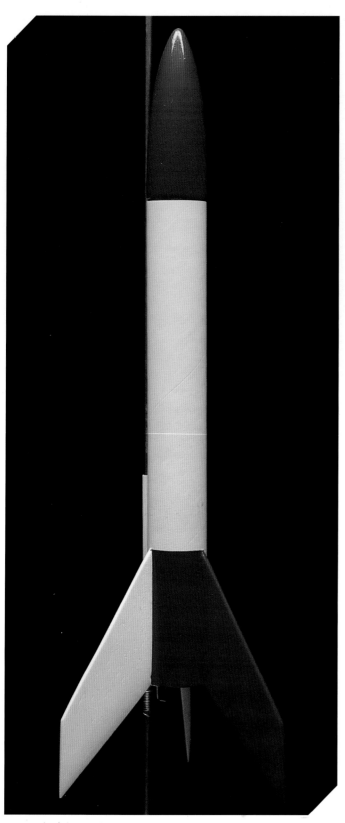

ALPHA
1967-2008

12.25 inches

ALPHA III
1971-PRESENT

12.25 inches

Alpha began production in 1967 with balsa fins and nose cone. Starting in 1971, there was both an Alpha and Alpha III in the catalog. Alpha and Alpha III were visually identical, but Alpha III has a plastic nose cone and fins for easier assembly. The same was true for Maxi Alpha and Maxi Alpha 3. There was an Alpha II, but it was a kit for educators.

TEROS
1973, 1977-82

Teros came out in 1973 as a cold-powered rocket (see "Cold-Powered Rockets" section in chapter 2), but it was convertible to a conventional pyro motor. It returned as a hot rocket in 1977. 13 inches.

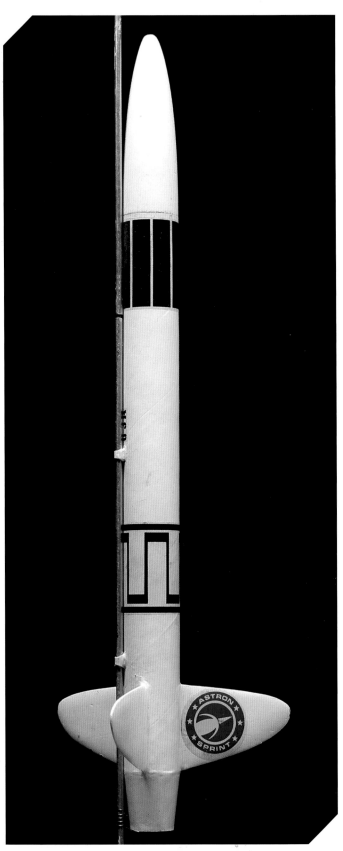

SPRINT
1969-70

Streamer recovery. The streamers created drag to slow the rocket. 13.8 inches.

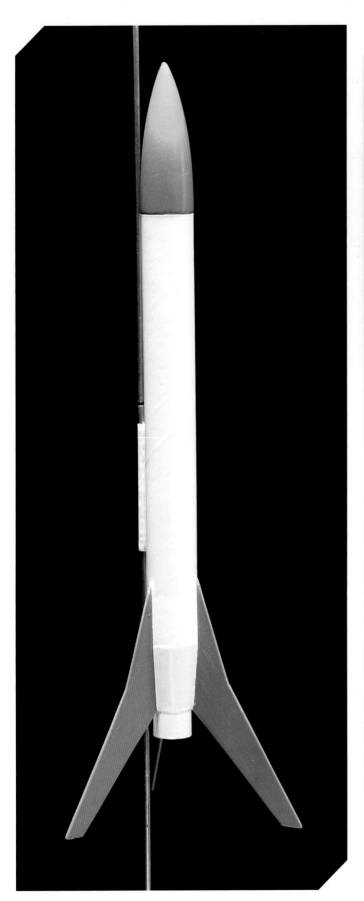

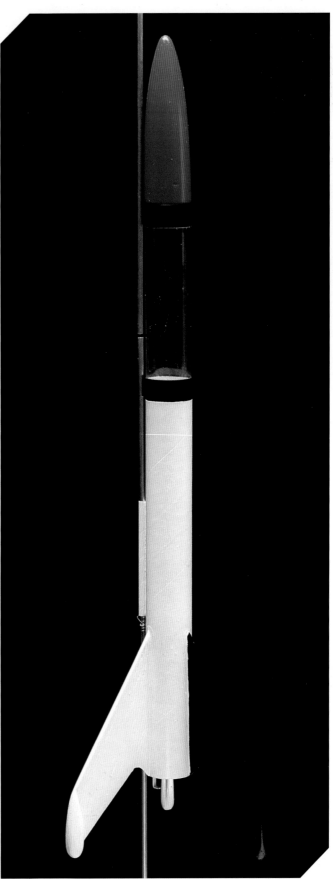

DRIFTER
1964-77
14.3 inches

Estes

CONSTELLATION
1969-78
16.2 inches

X-RAY
1966-85
16.75 inches

STARLIGHT
1968-72
18 inches

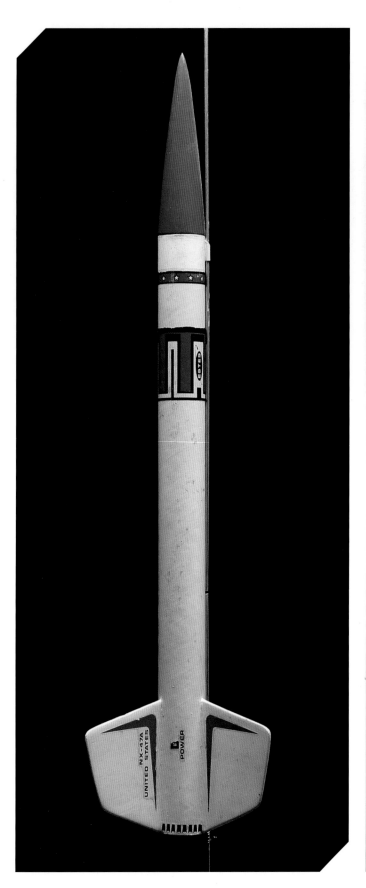

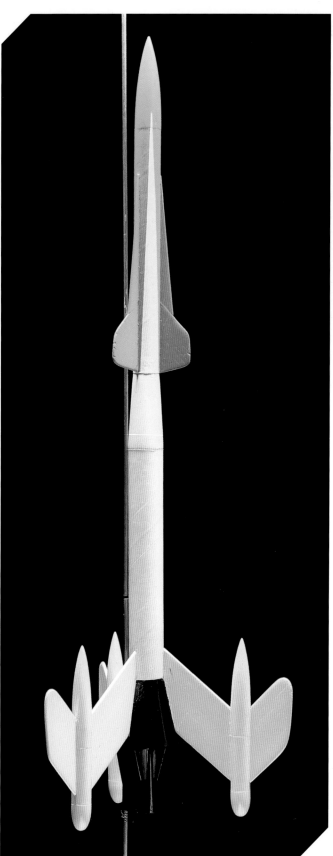

CHEROKEE-D
1971-82

D engine. 21.6 inches.

MARS SNOOPER
1966-74

Mars Snooper was somewhat revised in 1975 and released as "Mars Snooper II." It ran in that guise into the 1980s. 21.7 inches.

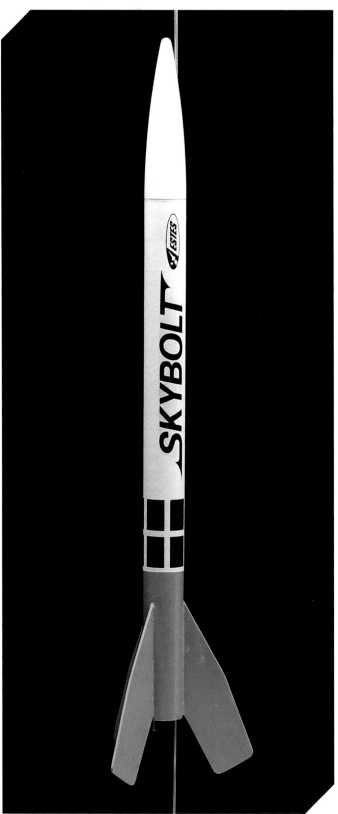

COBRA
1967-73

The Cobra contained a three-engine cluster. Getting all three engines to ignite simultaneously could be something of a challenge to rocketeers in the 1960s.
22.25 inches

SKYBOLT
1980-84

23 inches

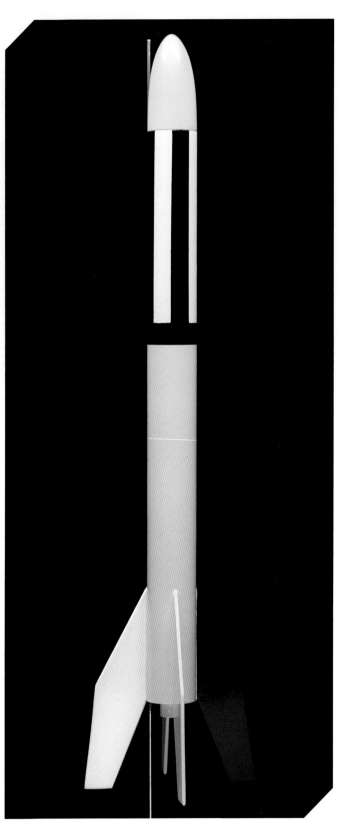

SCRAMBLER
1969-77

This was clearly designed as a challenge to see if you could fly an egg without breaking it. The Scrambler used a cluster of three engines to provide the power necessary to loft a relatively heavy payload. The stock fins were swept back; the egg shape fins on this one are custom built. 23.5 inches.

BIG BERTHA
1966-PRESENT

24.0 inches

CHALLENGER-II
1980-85
D–engine option. 24.25 inches.

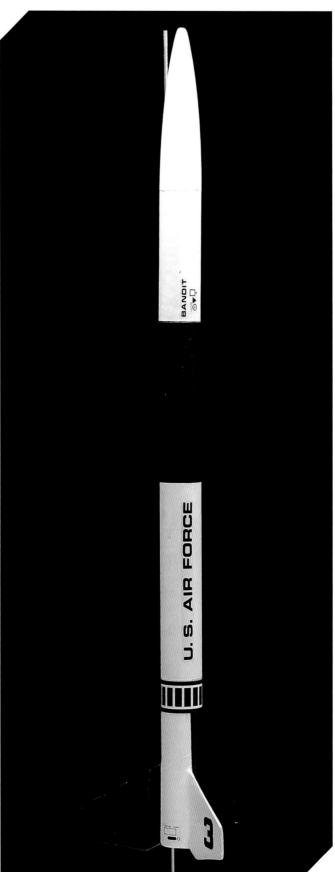

BANDIT
1972-82
25.75 inches

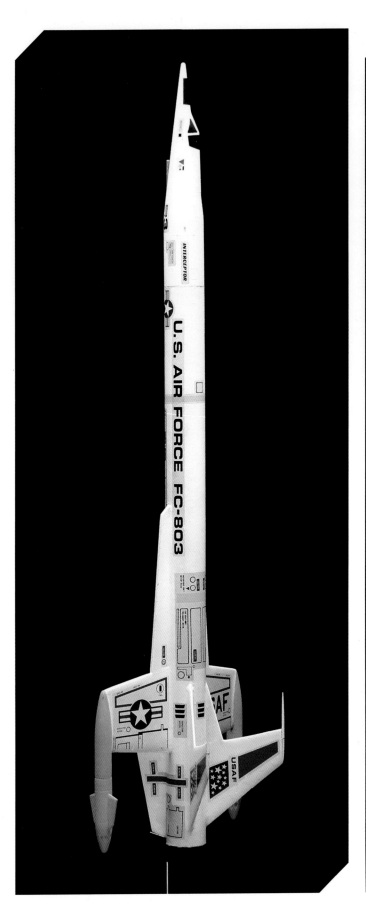

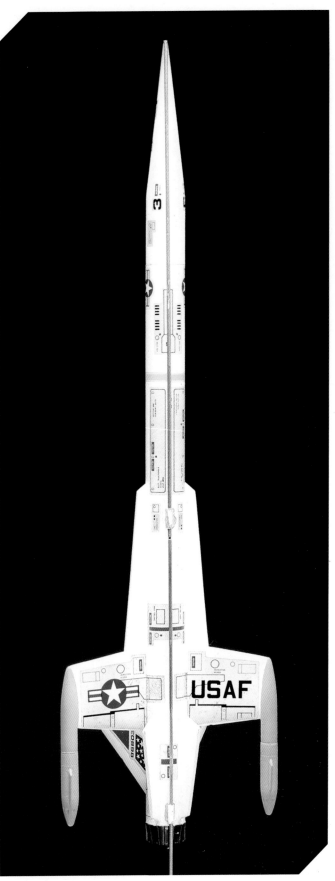

INTERCEPTOR
1971-80

26 inches

INTERCEPTOR
1971-80

26 inches

Estes

PATRIOT
1973-84
26 inches

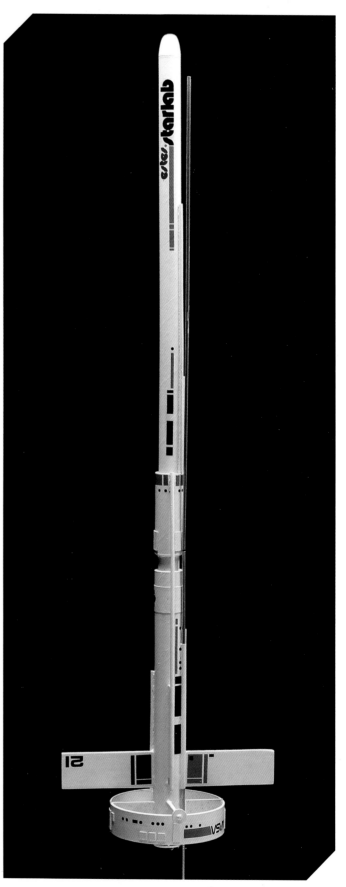

STARLAB
1977-80
27.75 inches

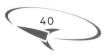

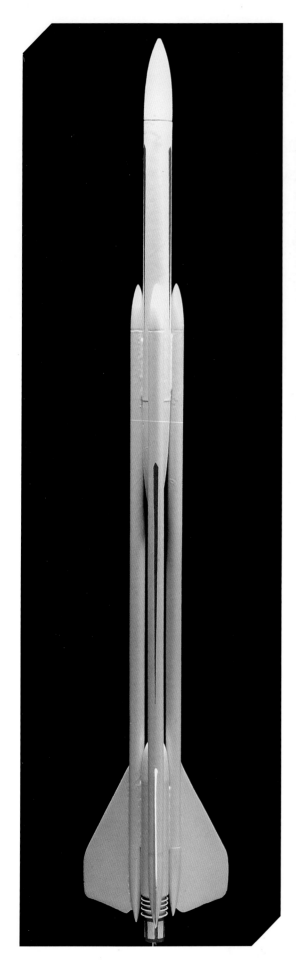

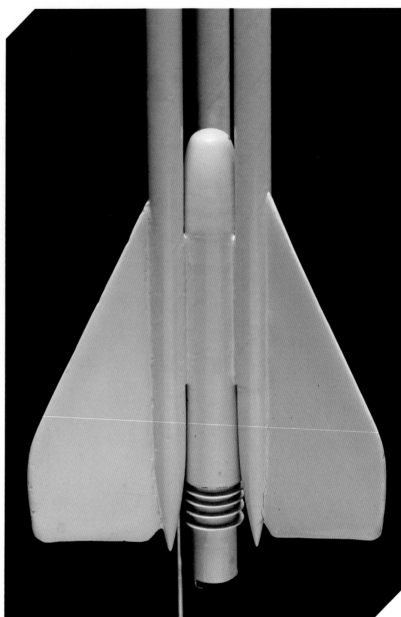

TRIDENT
1968-74

Trident was deceptively tricky to build. The motor ejection pulse had to go through the three tubes surrounding the engine and parachute tubes, requiring slits to be cut and carefully lined up between the central tubes and outer tubes. They had to be tightly glued to hold together upon ejection, but not with so much glue that it plugged the slits. My cousin was rightly proud of this model, and when he took it to show at the 1970 National Association of Rocketry (NAR) convention in Pittsburgh, the first thing he did going through the door was drop it and break a fin. In 1990, Estes came out with "Trident II," which had only two tubes. Strictly speaking, it should have been called "Bident." 31.6 inches.

SKY RAIDER
1977-83

D engine. 32.75 inches.

MAXI ALPHA
1977-85

D engine. 33.2 inches.

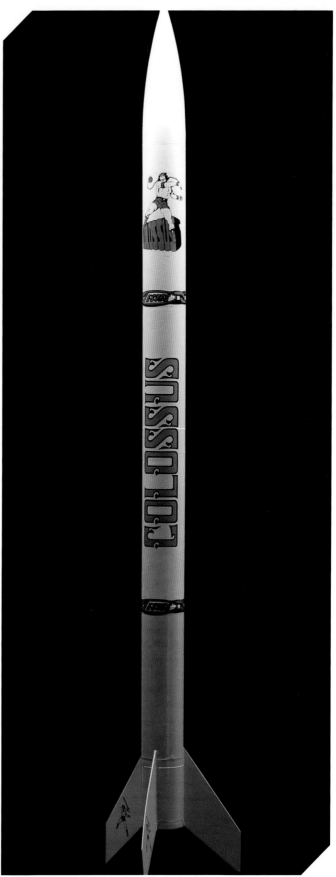

MAXI ALPHA 3
1979-85
D engine. 33.2 inches.

COLOSSUS
1979-83
D engine. 51.25 inches.

SANDPIPER
1972-75
Cold powered, 13.5 inches

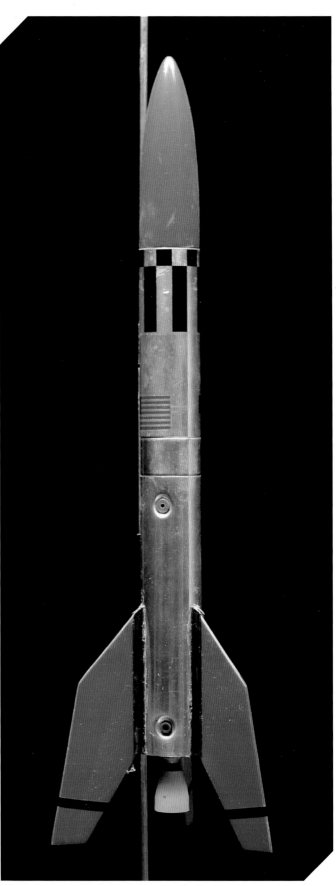

VALKYRIE I
1972-75
Cold powered, 14 inches

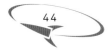

44

SCREAMIN' EAGLE
1975-77

These are horrid, terrible things that never should have been produced, and they deserved the quick death they got.

I had a Screamin' Eagle. Powered by a small cold-powered motor, it never went more than 10 feet and took its time getting there. I do not recall a drag chute, but I do recall never needing one. The wheels were open-cell foam rubber, the body was as thin as possible to save weight, and the whole thing had the stench of failure about it (though that might have been off-gassing from the foam rubber).

I used the motor as a proper rocket, launched on its own without even a nose cone or fins to its name. It performed much better in that service than in this abomination.

Cold powered, 11.4 inches

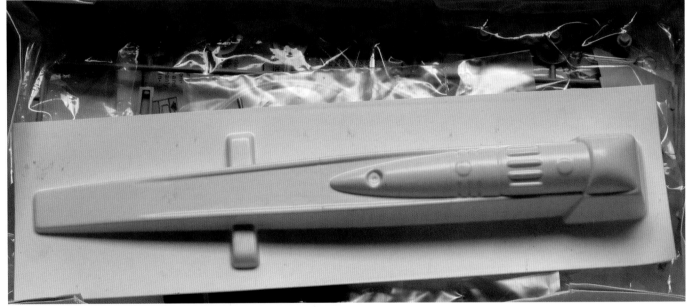

STARFIRE
1975-77
Cold powered, 13.25 inches

MULTISTAGE ROCKETS

Originally, Midget and Beta used short (S) engines. The Mini Engine versions were initially listed in the 1972 (721) catalog.

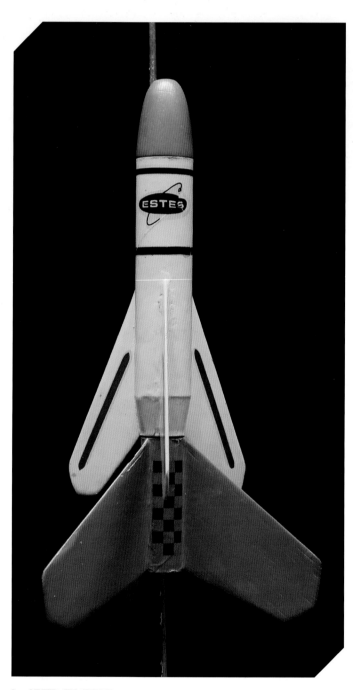

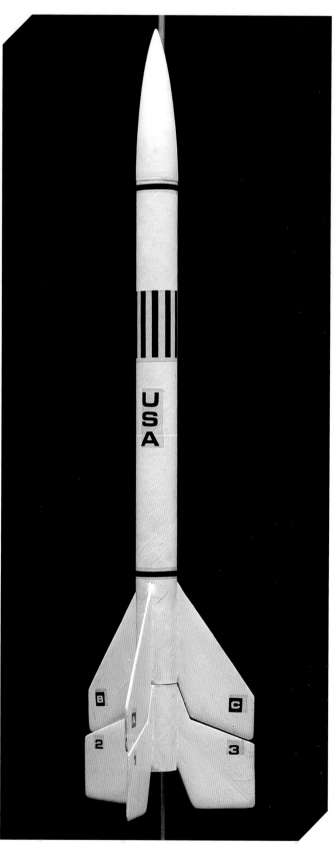

MIDGET
1969-73

As described under "Model Rocket design and Engine description," the lower-stage engines of multistage rockets did not have ejection charges. Instead, they fired sparks upward to ignite upper-stage engines. The lower stage gently flutters back to Earth. 9.25 inches.

BETA
1970-84

12.5 inches

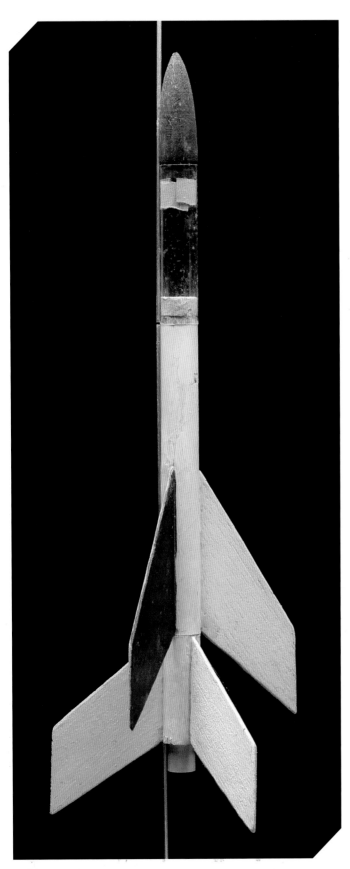

DELTA
1966-73

Delta was cataloged as a "workhorse booster" without a top. This one was built with a clear payload container. 13.6-inch body length without payload section.

APOGEE / APOGEE II
1963-81

Apogee was renamed Apogee II in 1964. There does not appear to be a difference between the two, and it probably was just to play up the two–stage feature of the rocket. 14.75 inches.

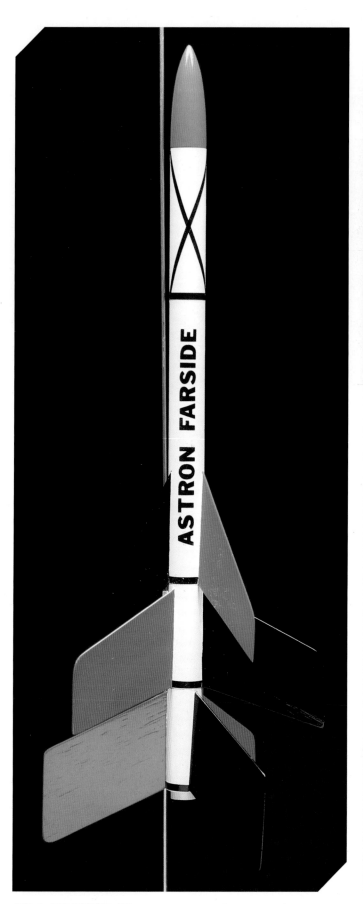

FARSIDE
1966-80
21.5 inches

SHRIKE
1970-79
29.5 inches

Estes

ROCKET PHOTOGRAPHY

AVENGER 1969-81

32 inches

Camroc was a nose cone camera that took a picture once it separated from the body of the carrier rocket. One of the challenges posed by the Camroc was selecting the proper time delay engine. If the modeler selected too short a delay, the camera would be pointed straight up when triggered.

Cineroc was a nose cone movie camera, which had to be turned on just before launch. The Super 8 mm movie cartridge held only enough film for twenty seconds, so you did not want to waste film waiting for liftoff. Its motor was powered by battery, but the drive mechanism was driven by a rubber belt, which could deteriorate, and the assembly was not designed for easy replacement.

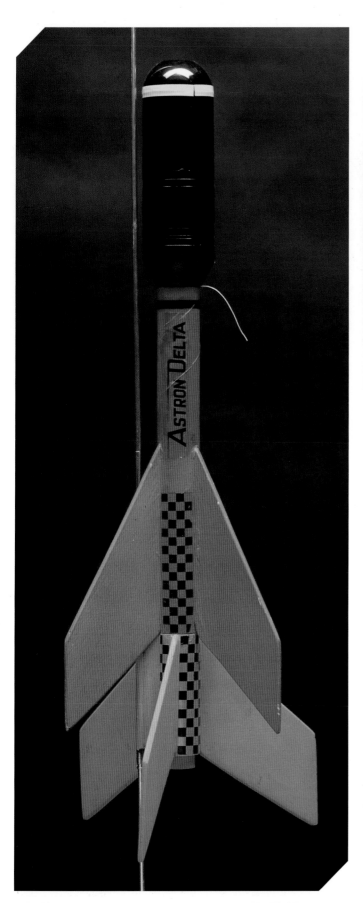

DELTA WITH CAMROC
1966-75

12.8 inches

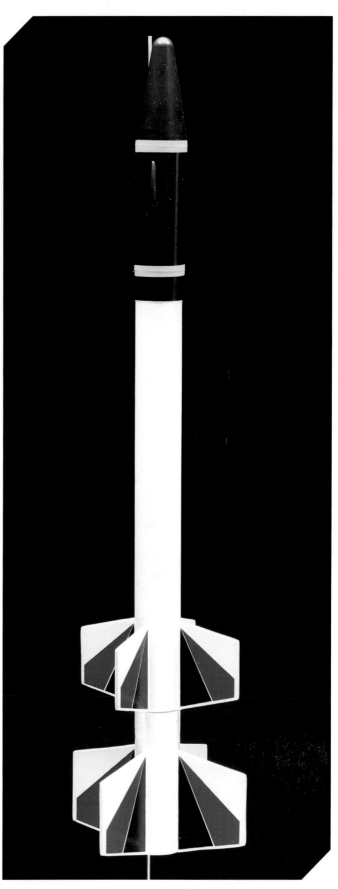

OMEGA WITH CINEROC
1970-75

30.5 in. (standard Omega length)

"GLIDERS"

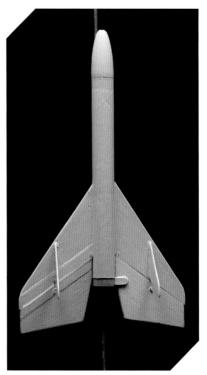

GYROC 1969-83

Admittedly, Gyroc isn't quite a glider, the way a helicopter isn't quite an airplane. When launched, flaps at the tips of the fins were locked in, parallel to the rocket body and in line with the fins. These flaps were held under tension with elastic threads. Upon engine ejection, the elevators were released and snapped over in opposing directions, making the rocket rotate. Gyroc landed by helicoptering back to Earth.

DELTA II WITH ASTROCAM 110 1979-91

AstroCam 110 took still pictures on 110 cartridge film. 19.1 inches.

Astron Gyroc

Whirly Bird **Rocket**

FASCINATING DESIGN

HELICOPTER RECOVERY

Excellent performance and amazing recovery system make the unique Gyroc a "bird" you'll want to own. Its unusual design gives this rocket the ability to reach high altitudes and return safely with helicopter recovery for minimum drift with wind. Comes complete with all instructions and parts. Engines not included. Shipping weight 5 oz. Cat. No. 671-K-24 . . . . $1.25

Specifications	Recommended Engines	
Weight . . . . 0.58 oz.	½A6-2	A8-3
Body Dia. . . 0.736 in.	B6-4	C6-5
Length . . . . . 9.8 in.		

LOW WIND DRIFT

9.8 inches

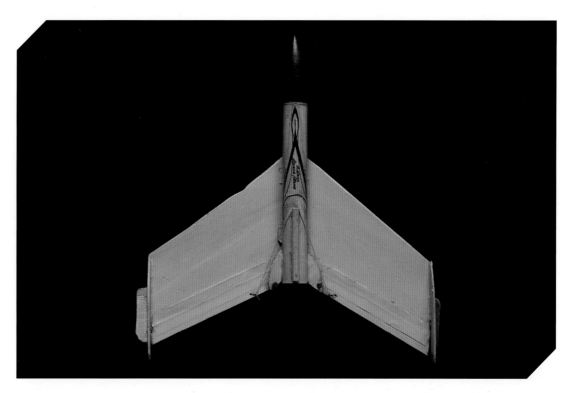

ASTRON

SPACE PLANE

Patent No. 3,157,960

SPACE PLANE
1963-71

Per the catalog, Space Plane "features easy and accurate adjustment of glide characteristics, plus a payload compartment large enough to handle small biological specimens and other scientific objects."

As a kid, I recall bigger kids putting small frogs ("biological specimens") into a clear payload compartment of a rocket. I do not recall any frogs getting hurt, but now as an adult, this seems like a cruel and pointless exercise. But cruel and pointless describes much of a young boy's childhood.

10 inches. 9-inch wingspan.

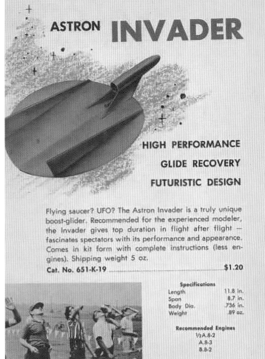

This lasted only one year in the catalog. Reportedly, it did not fly well. It doesn't look like it would.

INVADER
1966
11.8 inches

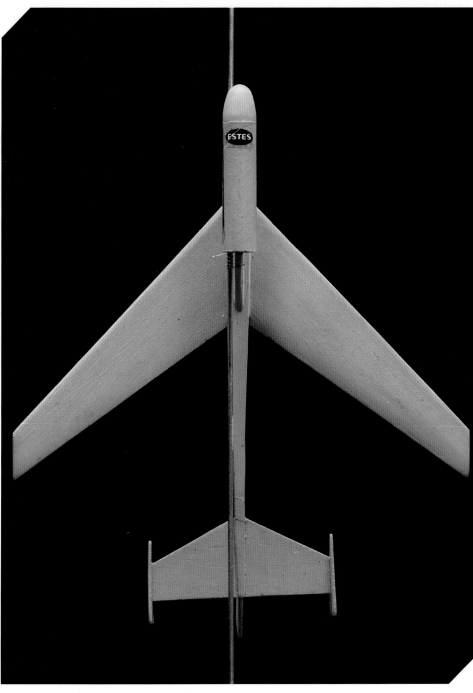
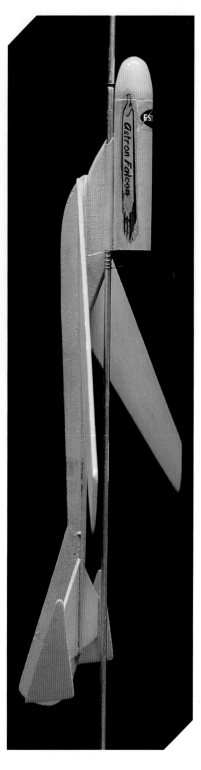

FALCON
1964-73
Falcon returns by ejecting its engine and becoming a glider. 12 inches. 10-inch wingspan.

Nighthawk separates on the ejection charge. The rocket end, or "power pod" according to the catalog, came down on a parachute while the glide vehicle "circles lazily against the blue sky."

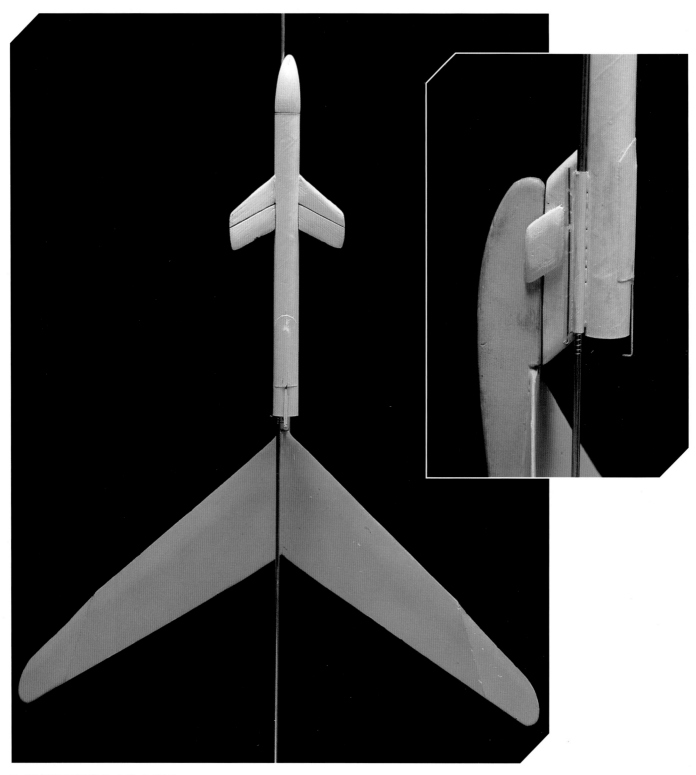

NIGHTHAWK
1968-73
Rocket power pod–glider attachment detail
19.75 inches. 16.25-inch wingspan.

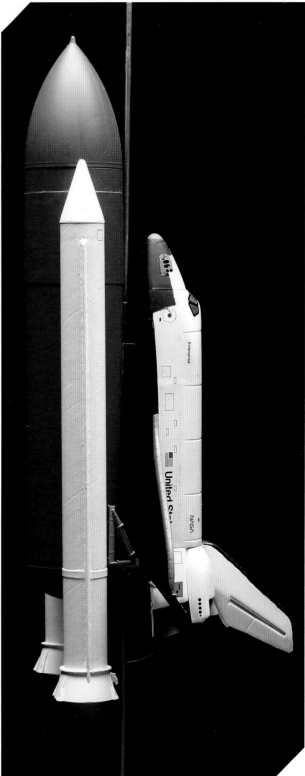

SPACE SHUTTLE
1976-98

The engine was in the main tank, and detachable finned tubes provided stability in flight. The vacu-formed plastic Orbiter separated and glided back. 13.6 inches. 9-inch orbiter wingspan.

SCISSOR WING TRANSPORT 1974-85

Scissor Wing Transport launched with a rubber band–loaded wing locked in the vertical position on the body. The engine was contained in a removable pod, which ejected out the back, releasing the wing. The wing swung out and the rocket glided back to Earth, with the pod returning via parachute.

22.75 inches. 16-inch wingspan.

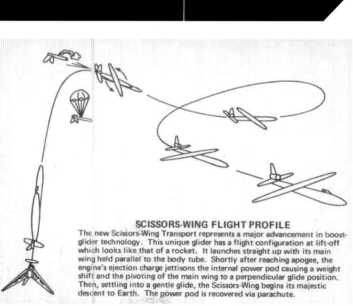

SCISSORS-WING FLIGHT PROFILE

The new Scissors-Wing Transport represents a major advancement in boost-glider technology. This unique glider has a flight configuration at lift-off which looks like that of a rocket. It launches straight up with its main wing held parallel to the body tube. Shortly after reaching apogee, the engine's ejection charge jettisons the internal power pod causing a weight shift and the pivoting of the main wing to a perpendicular glide position. Then, settling into a gentle glide, the Scissors-Wing begins its majestic descent to Earth. The power pod is recovered via parachute.

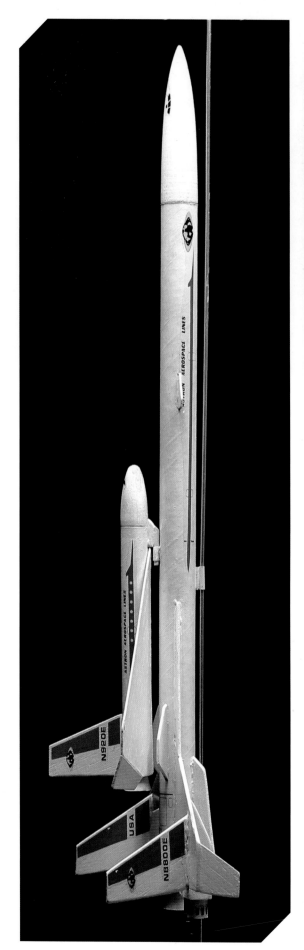

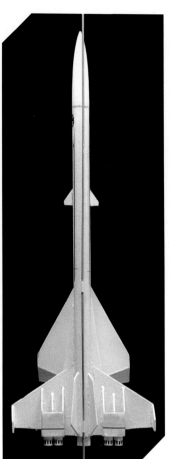

ORBITAL TRANSPORT 1969-85

The shock of the ejection charge for the parachutes kicks off the reentry vehicle. 23-inch booster. 8.6-inch reentry vehicle.

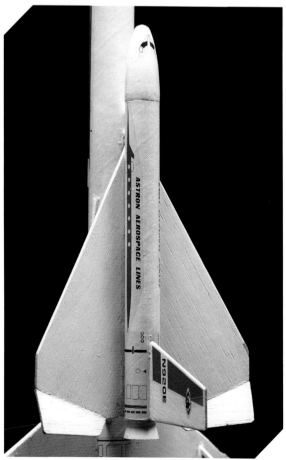

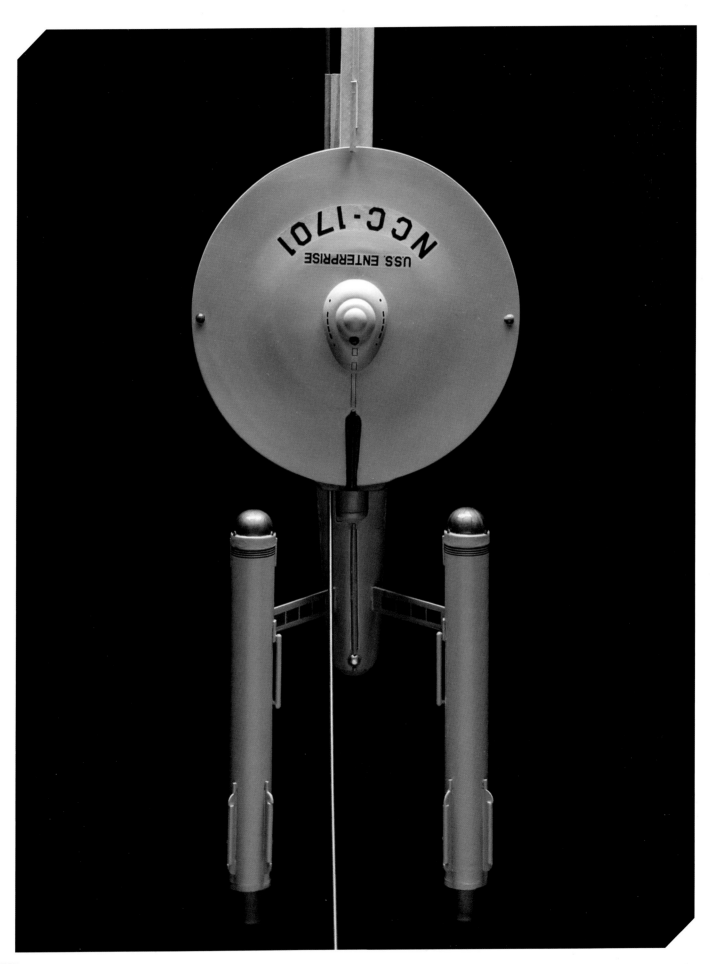

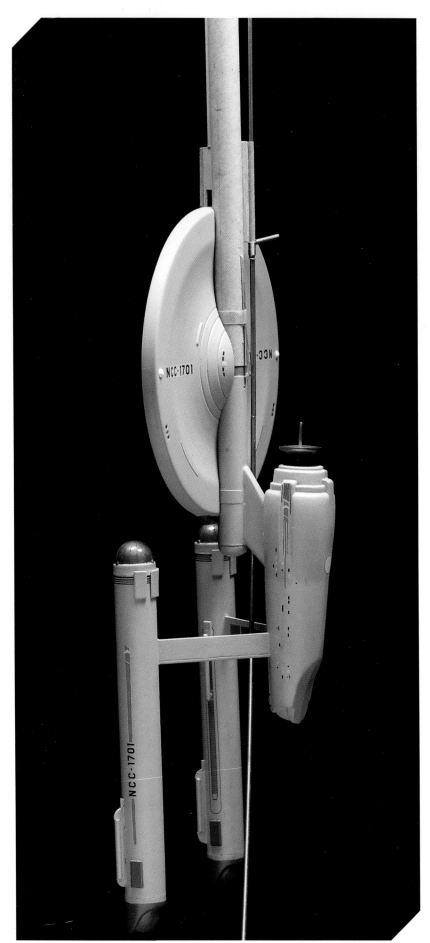

STAR TREK / STAR WARS

ENTERPRISE
1975-79

The very long, unpainted cardboard tube is what Estes called a "parachute recovery probe" and is attached for flight. 16.8 inches.

Estes

61

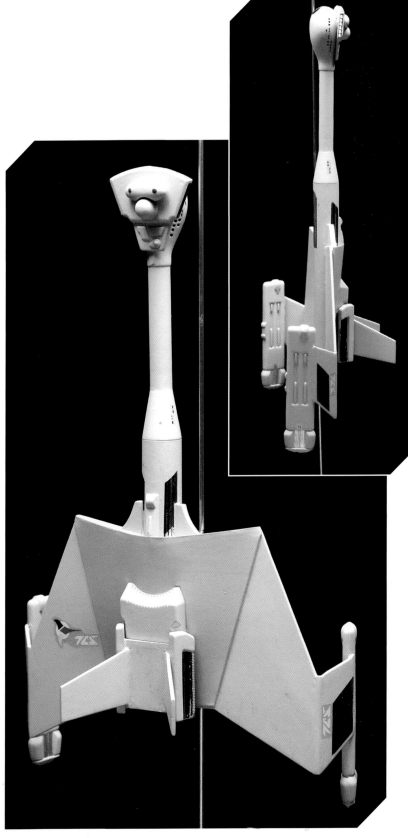

STAR TREK
1977-78

This rocket goes to a Star Trek starter kit and was not available for separate sale. A different set of graphics were used on the 1976 version. 12.0 inches.

KLINGON CRUISER
1975-79

15.1 inches

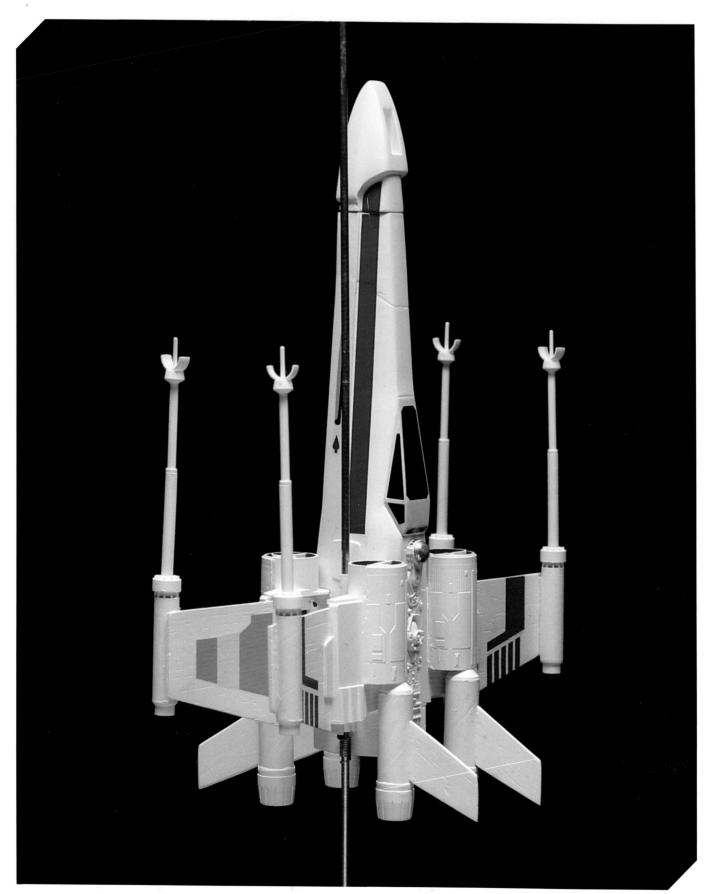

X-WING FIGHTER
1979-98
10.9 inches

Estes

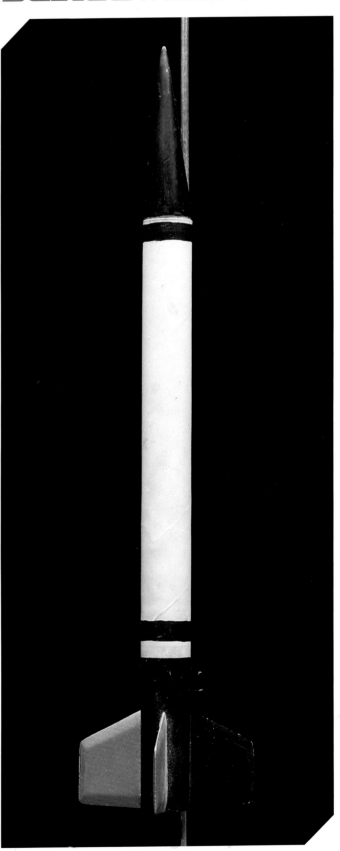

SCALE MODELS

V-2
1966-77
11.2 inches

WAC CORPORAL
1964-77
11.8 inches

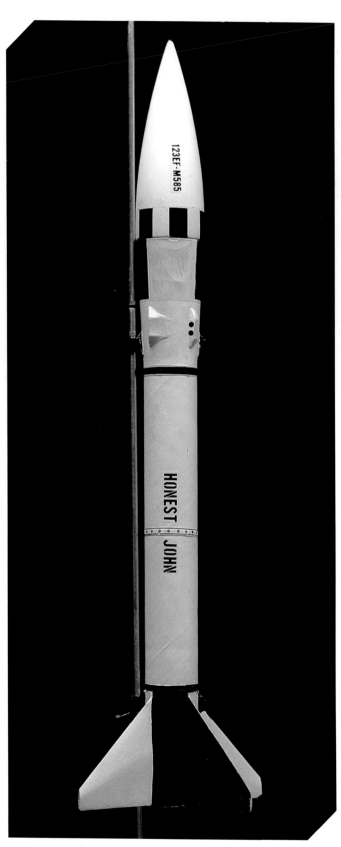

Thor Agena B came with a slip-on clear-plastic fin assembly for stable flight. The same is true for the Gemini-Titan rocket.

HONEST JOHN
1967-79

The nose cone is separated into two pieces: the lower piece is a paper shroud connected to the body; the upper piece is balsa. Centuri also made an Honest John with a one-piece balsa nose cone.
13.75 inches

THOR AGENA-B
1967-71

17.25 inches

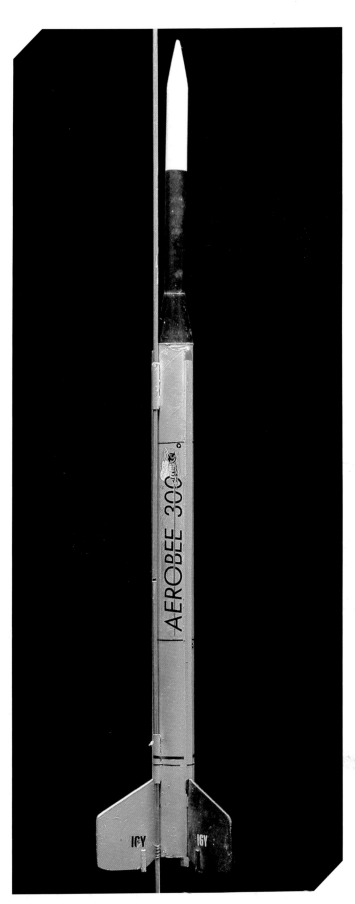

AEROBEE 300
1965-78

20 inches

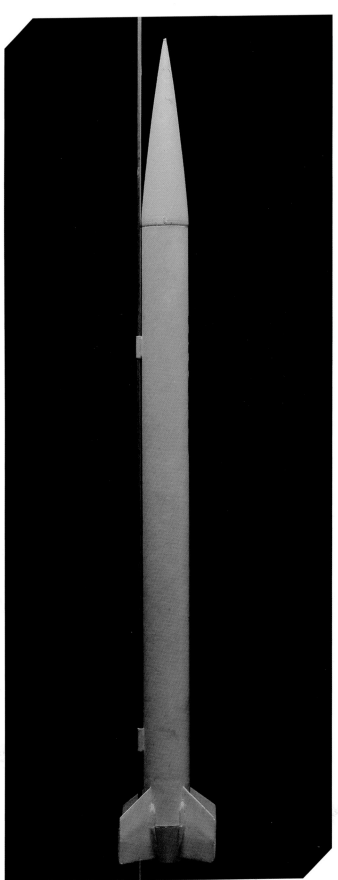

ARCAS
1966-77

22.8 inches

66

NIKE-X
1975-84
23.4 inches

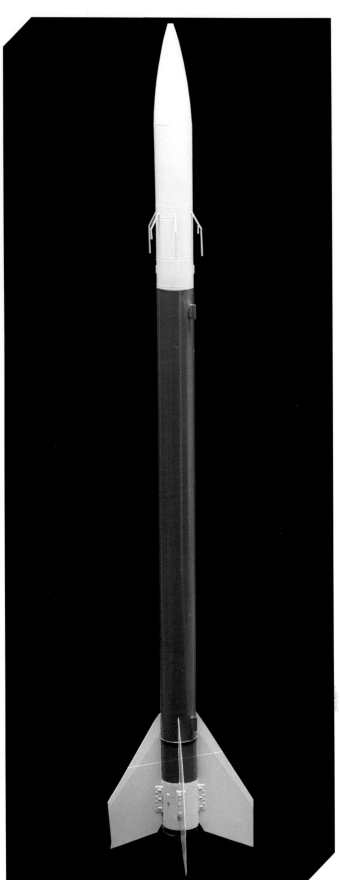

SANDHAWK
1971-79
D-engine option, 30.1 inches

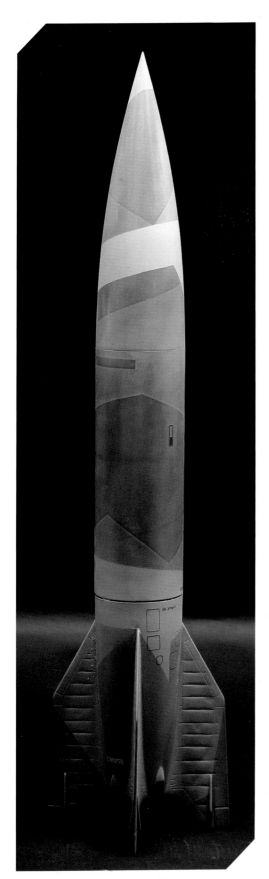

V-2 MAXI BRUTE
1974–81

D engine, 33.5 inches

HONEST JOHN
MAXI BRUTE
1975–82

D engine, 37 inches

PERSHING 1-A
MAXI BRUTE
1974–82

D engine, 41 inches

NASA SERIES

Little Joe II was as a test vehicle for the Apollo spacecraft launch escape system.

This model is 1:70 scale. A smaller 1:100 Little Joe was released in 1991.

LITTLE JOE II
1968-71

14.5 inches

Estes

SATURN V SEMI-SCALE
1969-79

18.1 inches

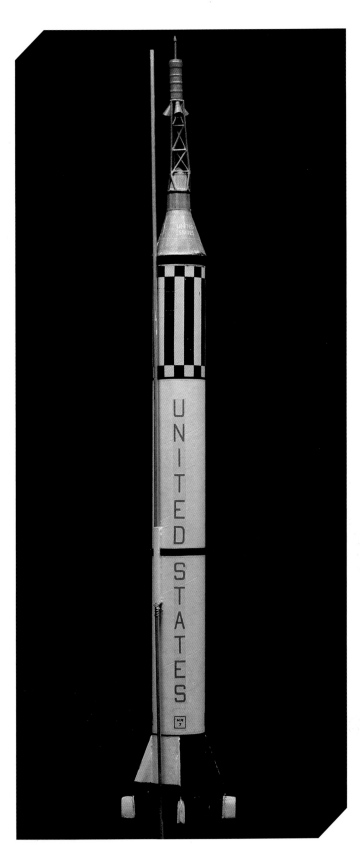

MERCURY REDSTONE
1969-90

Detail showing paper-wrapped capsule and wooden dowel tower, which had to be assembled piece by piece. It was also cataloged as a separate sale item. A post–1980 version of Mercury Redstone was a complete redesign; it came with a plastic capsule and was slightly bigger.

23.5 inches

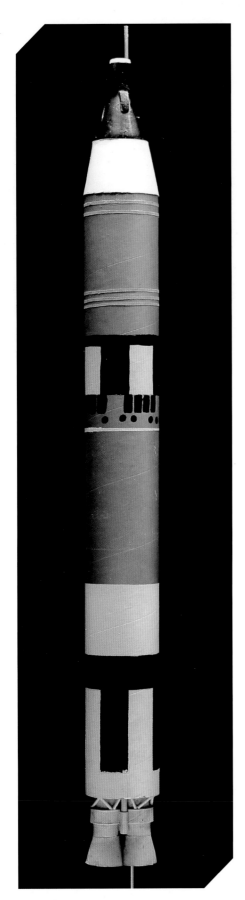

GEMINI-TITAN
1968-88

Dual motor. 24.4 inches.

SATURN 1B
1967-77

Four-engine cluster. 37 inches.

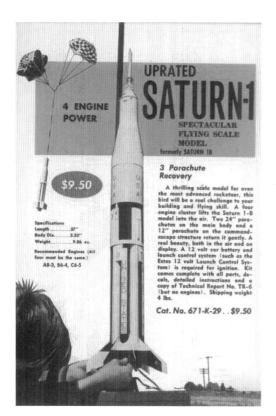

This is Estes' most ambitious rocket. The 1967–77 Saturn 1–B was 1:70 scale, larger in scale than the 1:100 Saturn V rocket that Estes introduced in 1969. The Saturn 1–B was a large and challenging model to build.

Saturn 1–B has no plastic parts. The tower, thrusters, and associated details are made from stock wood and card stock. Paper shrouding had to be cut and wrapped around the multiple external tanks.

The fins—there are eight of them—are balsa skeletons covered with cardstock. Flying this model farther represented a challenge for most rocketeers because it used a cluster of four engines, all of which had to ignite simultaneously for a successful flight.

Estes released a smaller 1:100 scale, skill level 4 Saturn 1–B in 1991, which was based on a Centuri model.

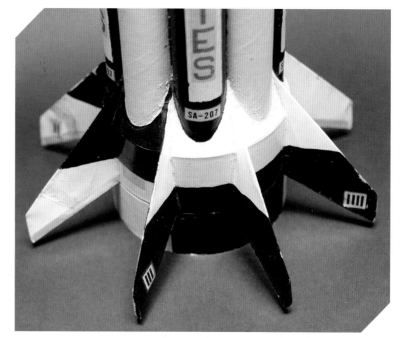

The Apollo capsule was also available for separate sale and could be built for display or separate launching with a motor adapter. Like the Mercury capsule, the escape tower is built from individual wooden dowels.

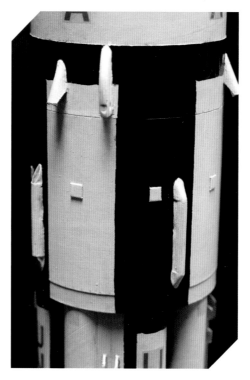

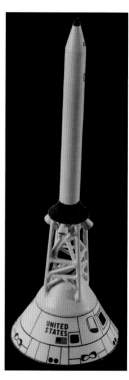

SATURN V 1969-2019

The 1:100 scale Saturn V is Estes' flagship model, and it was in the catalog for decades. This is the original 1969 version.

The rocket nozzles were plastic models for display. For flight, they are removed and either three C engines or a single D engine is installed. Slip-on plastic fins go over the balsa fins, which are scale in size but too small for model rocket stability. The real Saturn V's nozzles were gimbal mounted to maintain directional control.

In 2021, a 1:100 model returned with a Skylab payload instead of Apollo.

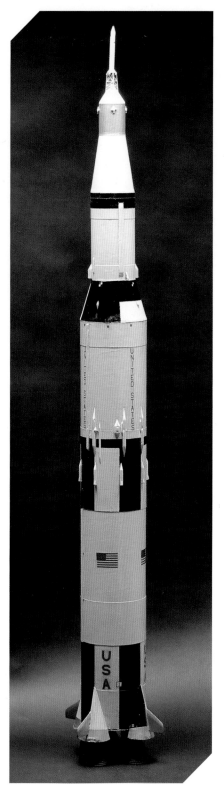

Three-engine-cluster D-motor option. 43.5 inches.

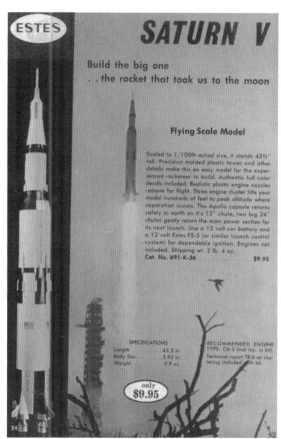

1969 catalog, $9.95

Saturn V as cataloged, showing effects of inflation over eleven years

1980 catalog, $28.95

CENTURI

Leroy E. (Lee) Piester started Centuri in Phoenix, Arizona, in 1961 as a direct competitor to Estes. To gain a performance advantage, in 1963, Centuri bought the Coaster Company, which had been making powerful rocket motors. The company was absorbed into the Phoenix operation, and the 1964 Centuri catalog listed Coaster's high-powered motor, high-performance Aero-Dart rocket kit, a launchpad to handle it, and an assortment of parts for large models.

The 1965 Centuri catalog included ex-Coaster "E" (Atlas) and "F" (Hercules) motors. Atlas has low thrust with long burn time, whereas Hercules had high thrust with short burn time. Other large model rocket kits were introduced (Scorpion, Explorer, and Hustler). In 1967, this large-scale line was rebranded Mini-Max.

While this was going on, a company called Rocket Development Corporation (RDC), owned by Irv Wait of Seymour, Indiana, developed a motor charged with composite propellant instead of traditional black powder. It has three times the energy density of black powder. Seeing a good fit with its high-performance line, Centuri bought RDC in 1969.

Piester sold the company to Damon Industries, owners of Estes, in 1970. On paper, Centuri bought out Estes so that the company was located in tax-advantaged Arizona instead of Colorado. Centuri manufacturing slowly moved to Penrose, Colorado, with the Arizona operation involved in marketing and warehousing.

The lines were kept separate until 1976 and often overlapped in the scale model series. Centuri kits used more plastic with higher detailing than Estes. Some, such as a 1:36 scale Mercury-Redstone and 1:45 scale Little Joe II, were larger, and most were more expensive than their Estes counterparts. In the case of the Saturn rockets, they were significantly so. For example, Centuri's 1974 Saturn V was an ambitious $24.95, whereas Estes was a more obtainable $16.95.

In 1974, Lee Piester was listed as Centuri president and was still greeting kids in the full-color Centuri catalog. By 1975 the catalog was reduced to a black-and-white newspaper format, though Evel Knievel's rocket was in color, with a greeting by Charles Fox, the Centuri general manager. The line merged with Estes in 1976.

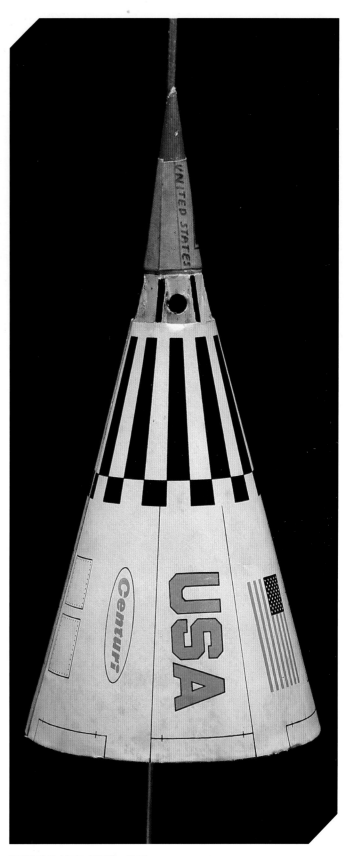

STAR TROOPER
1974-79
Streamer recovery (rear ejected). 5.6 inches.

THE POINT
1969-71
Rigid chute recovery (body acts as parachute). 8.1 inches.

Billed in the catalog as the "World's smallest 2-stage rocket," and so it was, pipping the Estes Astron Midget by 0.25 inches.

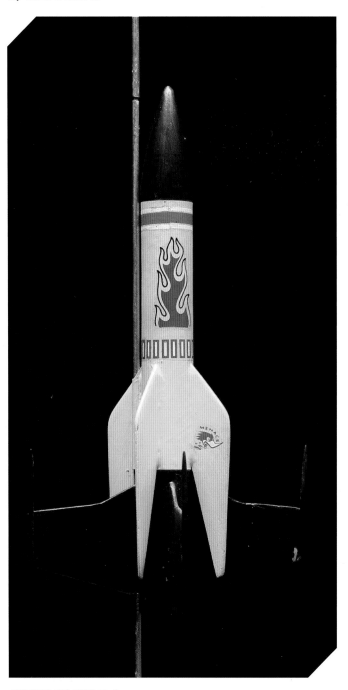

FIREFLY
1969-71
Streamer recovery. 9.0 inches.

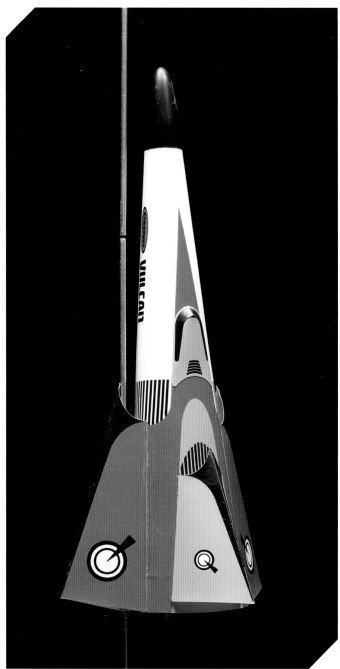

VULCAN
1972-79
10.5 inches

The large booster-stage fins are to provide lift to glide the stage back to Earth.

The inky-black void of space background just wasn't going to work for this one.

BLACK WIDOW
1962-79

18.0 inches

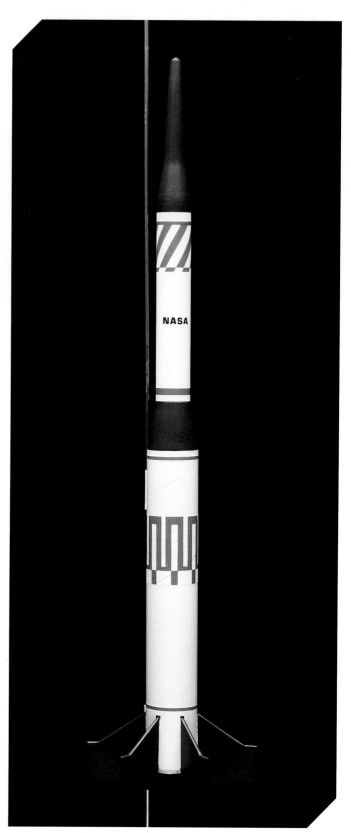

RECRUITER
1967-71

19.0 inches

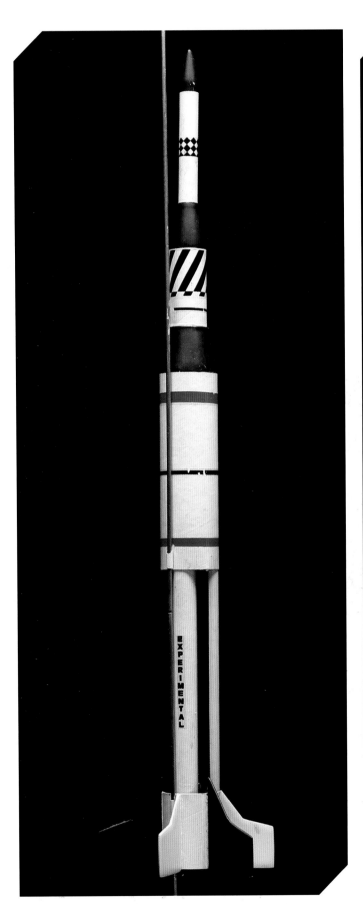

DEFENDER
1968-69

Three-engine power. 21.0 inches.

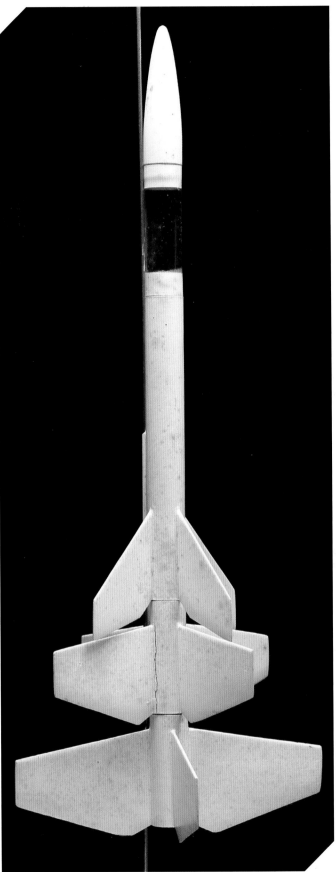

T BIRD
1968-75

21.3 inches

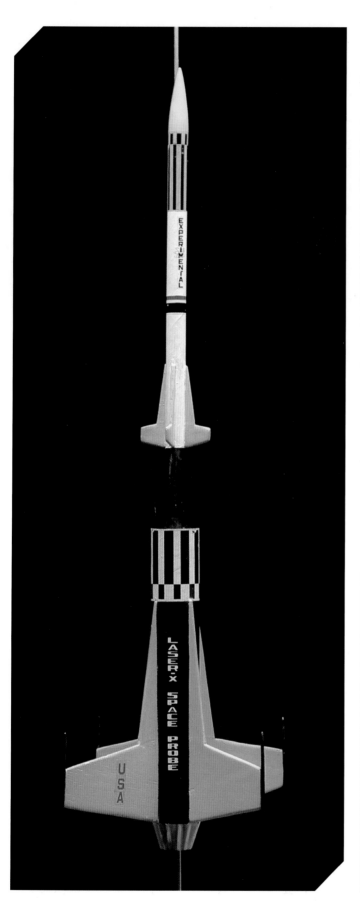

LASER-X
1969-81

21.5 inches

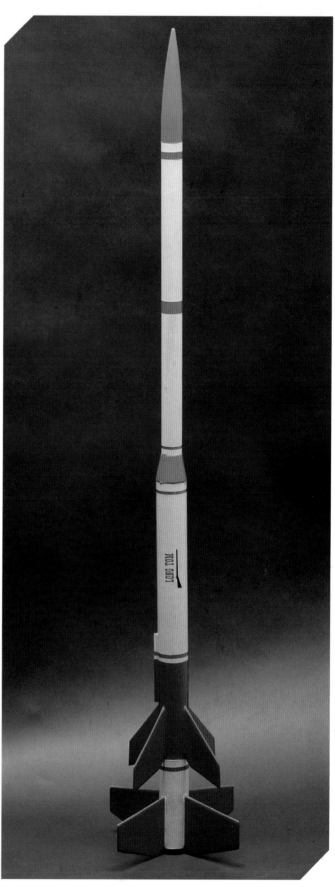

LONG TOM
1971-81

36.5 inches

Centuri

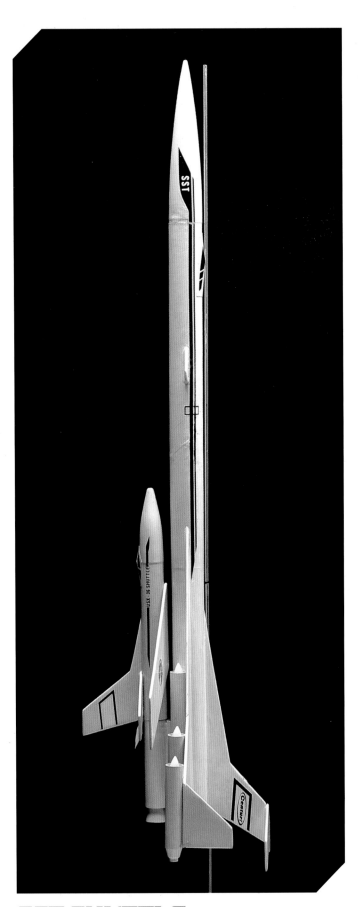

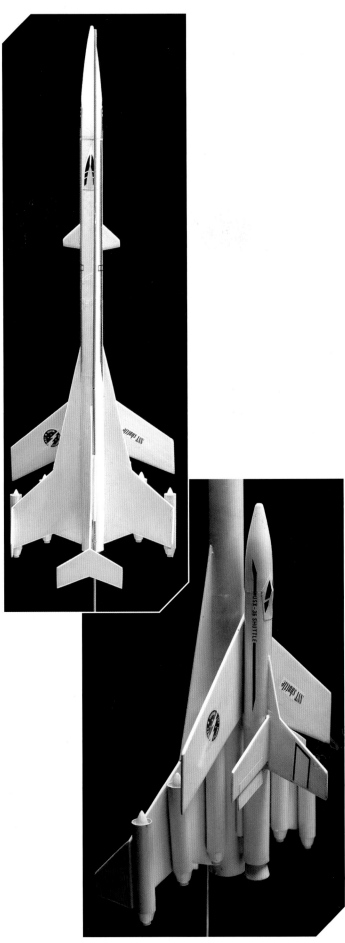

SST SHUTTLE
1971-82

SST carried a glider that released upon ejection charge. 22.5 inches.

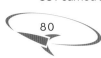

SUPER-SCALE SERIES

Centuri's catalog claimed superiority in design and construction with their Super Scales model rocket line, and the 1969 $15.95 price of their Saturn V over Estes' $9.95 version reflected it.

Other rockets in the scale series were either significantly more expensive than the Estes counterparts, though somewhat bigger, or price competitive, though somewhat smaller.

1969 catalog

CHAPTER 5

OTHER MANUFACTURERS

MPC, known for their plastic model car kits, obtained MRI in 1969 and were in the rocket business until 1973, when they sold it to Aerospace Vehicles Inc. (AVI). Unsurprisingly, MPC used a lot of plastic in their rockets.

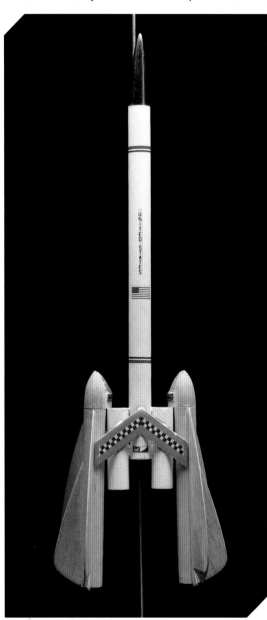

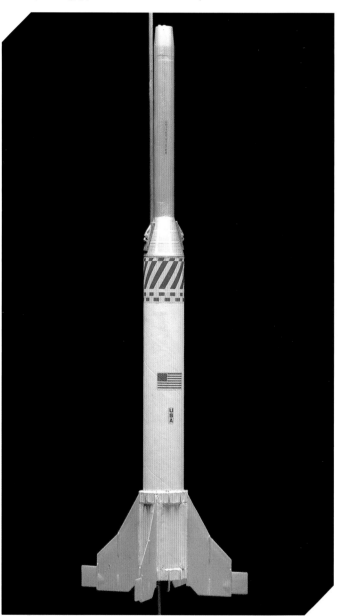

LUNAR PATROL
1969-73, MPC
This rocket contained two gliders, which it shrugged off upon ejection. 15.0 in. rocket, 7.0 in. gliders.

REDSTONE MAVERICK
1969-73, MPC
16.0 inches

MPC produced this 1:100 scale plastic kit that could be converted to a flying rocket with a cardboard engine insert, which prevented melting from hot gases and contained a parachute. The capsule is clear on one side to show details of the inner command and reentry module.

VOSTOK (BOCTOK)
1969-73, MPC

15.0 inches

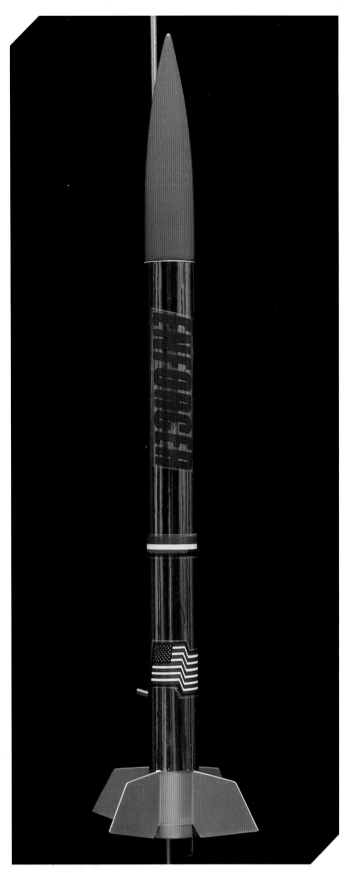

ENFORCER
CA. 1970, MRC
15.08 inches

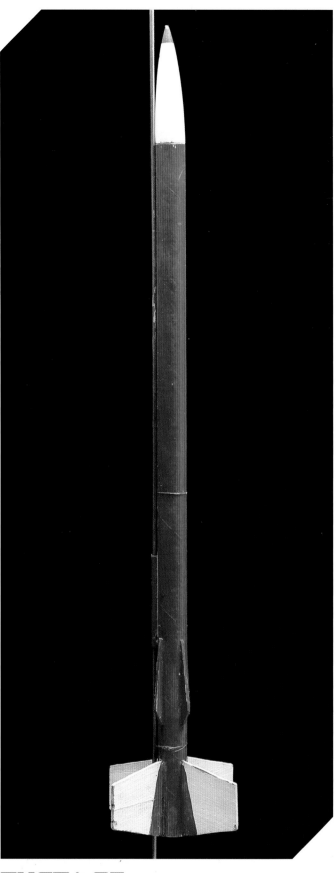

THETA 37
CA. 1969 MODEL ROCKET INDUSTRIES [MRI]
21.0 inches

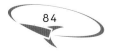

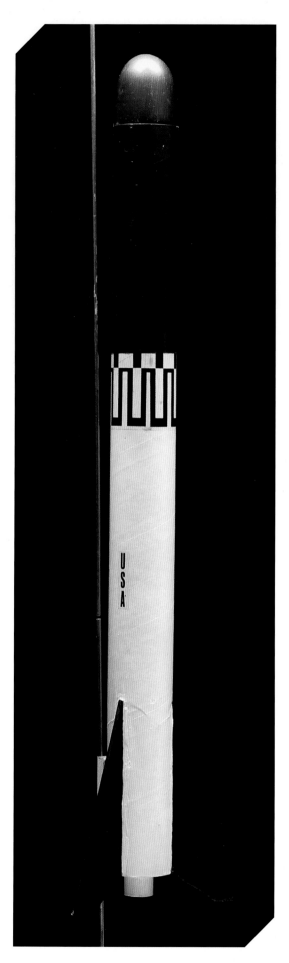

KOPTER
CA. 1976, KOPTER ROTOR
RECOVERY ROCKETS

Kopter Rotary Recoverable Rockets was a Pittsburgh–based company that, by its name, appears to have been in business to promote rotary recovery in rockets. The catalog proudly displays the patent for the device (patent no. 3,903,801: granted 1975, expired 1992).

Despite all the hoopla over the recovery method, the rocket shown is the only rotary recoverable rocket in a catalog containing nineteen rockets. The rest had streamer recovery or were gliders. There was a rotary option for recovery of an ejectable engine pod for one of their gliders.

When this one was flown, a blade was damaged when it hit a fin. It helicoptered back, but a little off-balance due to the damage.

Estes later adopted rotary recovery in the Skywinder rocket, first cataloged in 1993.

Helicopter recovery. 22 inches.

CHAPTER 6

ROCKETS FROM PLANS

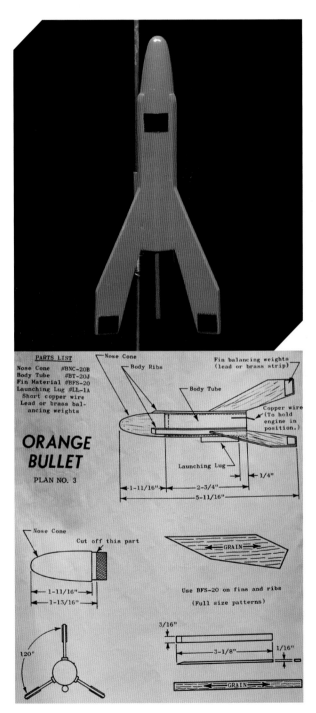

PARTS LIST
Nose Cone   #BNC-20B
Body Tube   #BT-20J
Fin Material #BFS-20
Launching Lug #LL-1A
Short copper wire
Lead or brass bal-
ancing weights

Nose Cone
Body Ribs
Body Tube
Fin balancing weights
(lead or brass strip)
Copper wire
(To hold
engine in
position.)
Launching Lug
1/4"

ORANGE BULLET
PLAN NO. 3

1-11/16"   2-3/4"
5-11/16"

Nose Cone
Cut off this part
GRAIN

1-11/16"
1-13/16"

Use BFS-20 on fins and ribs
(Full size patterns)

120°

3/16"
3-1/8"   1/16"
GRAIN

ORANGE BULLET
1966

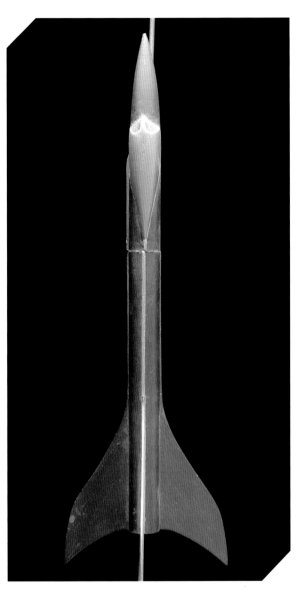

STAR BLAZER
1968

The Star Blazer was first offered as a free kit as a customer reward for orders over $5.00. In 1970 it was added to the catalog. The Star Blazer didn't remain in the Estes product line for long; 1971 was the only other year this kit was offered. In its original form the Star Blazer used the short engines, so when Estes discontinued them in favor of the Mini Engines, engines for the Star Blazer were no longer available. In 1972, Estes recycled the name for a completely different rocket that used Mini Engines. 12.5 inches.

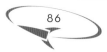

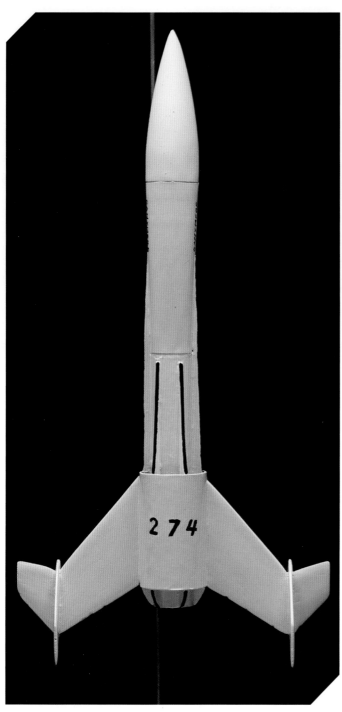

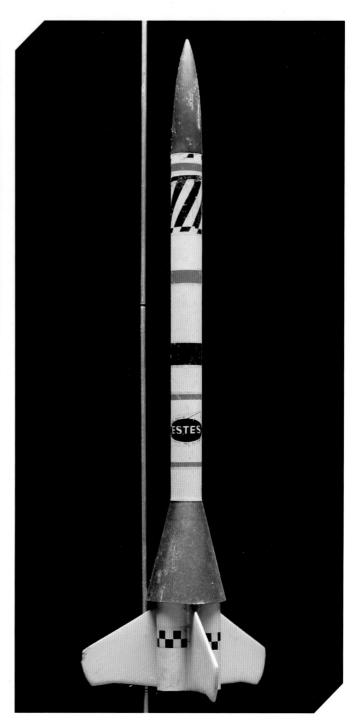

GANYMEDE 274
1969

Built from Estes Rocket Plan 59 in *Model Rocket News* 9, no. 1 (1969). 14.9 inches.

SCOTT-B
1969

Built from the Estes Rocket Plan 66, design of the month in *Model Rocket News* 9, no. 3 (1969). Despite appearances, it had only a single rocket motor in the first stage. 14.9 inches.

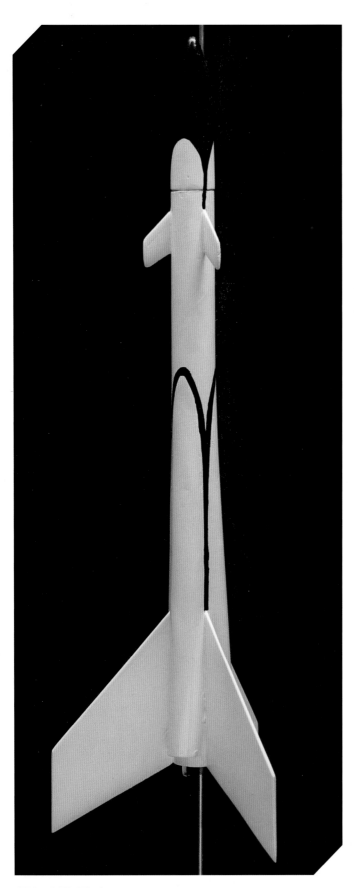

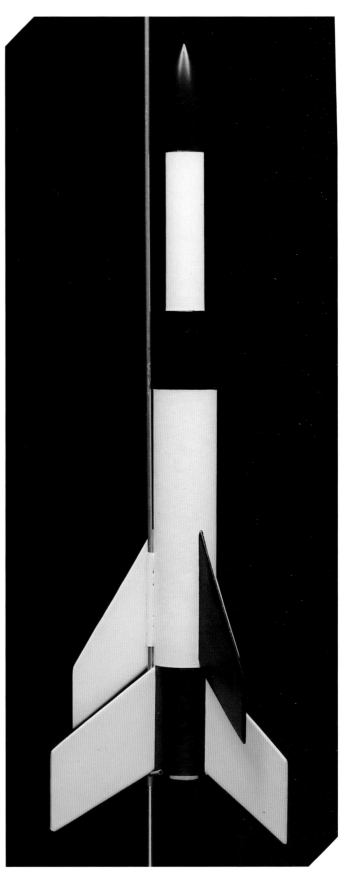

OMEGA
1969

Built from Estes Rocket Plan 63 in *Model Rocket News* 9, no. 3 (1969). 17.5 inches.

CHALLENGER
1967

Built from Estes Rocket Plan 51, *Model Rocket News* 7, no. 1 (1967). 19.7 inches.

STARSHIP EXCALIBUR
1968

Starship Excalibur was built in period from Estes Industries Rocket Plan 55 in *Model Rocket News*. 8, no. 2 (1968). It came out as a kit in 1984. 20.5 inches.

CHAPTER 7

LAUNCHERS

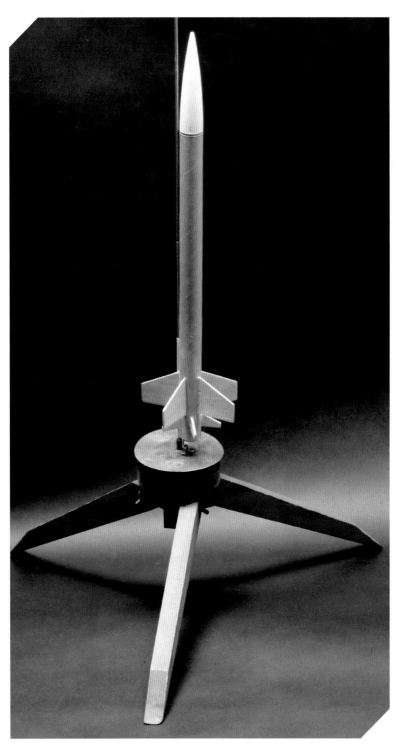

**ESTES TILT-
A-PAD
1964-78**

90

ESTES ELECTRO-LAUNCH 1964-71

1968 Electro–Launch

Page 48

ELECTRO LAUNCH

- Dependable
- Convenient
- Portable
- Compact

Only $3.00 P.P.
Cat. No. 641-FS-1
(without batteries)

Fly your rockets the "professional" way with this completely self-contained launching system. Engineered for simplicity, safety, dependability, and convenience, the Electro-Launch is a basic piece of equipment for model rocketeers. Collapsible 36" long two-piece launching rod guides light weight models into the air for accurate flights. Use it for rockets weighing up to 6 oz., or anchor the base to the ground for heavier models. Spring return safety switch permits safe loading of rockets on launcher. Uses 4 size D photoflash batteries (#PFB-1). For heavy duty use the addition of a battery pack (#BP-1) is recommended to give longer battery life and sure starts in cold weather.

Complete with all parts and instructions, but no batteries. Shipping weight 50 ounces.

Complete Electro-Launch kit also available with 4 batteries. Special price $4.00.

OR--Get the same kit as above, but complete with batteries: Cat. No 641-FS-1B $4.00 P.P.

Page 49

ASTRO-LAUNCH
ULTIMATE in UTILITY and CONVENIENCE

Now a truly universal rocket launching system. Use it with car batteries, hot shot batteries, a pair of #BP-1 battery packs, or any other 6 or 12 volt high current power source. Combine it with the new Tilt-A-Pad for complete mobility! Key safety switch prevents accidental launchings, combination arm and continuity check light helps eliminate misfires--lights only when the safety switch is on and the micro-clips make a good connection to the igniter. Extra large battery clips attach firmly to almost any battery. Unit comes completely assembled with 25 feet of lead wire. Available for 6 or 12 volt power supplies. Specify voltage when ordering. Shipping weight 1 pound 6 ounces.

Cat. No. 641-FS-3 $6.50 each

Astro-Launch Panel

Combine the compactness and portability of the Electro-Launch with the complete control of the Astro-Launch!

This compact panel attaches easily to your Electro-Launch in place of the standard switch. You get the same continuity check, key control, etc., as in the Astro-Launch, but without wires and clips. Available for use with either 6 or 12 volts. Specify voltage when ordering. Panel comes pre-assembled, ready to connect and use. Shipping weight 8 ounces.
Cat. No. 641-FS-2 $4.50 each

Replaces spring switch on any ELECTRO LAUNCH

1964 Electro-Launch. Early Electro-Launches were somewhat agricultural. Later ones were more refined.

This is the classic rocket launcher. Porta–Pad was replaced with the similar Porta–Pad II in 1989. Shown in Estes Power–pulse™ launch controller using Polaroid's Polapulse™ P100 battery pack. The pack was originally developed for their cameras, but this was an attempt by Polaroid to expand the market for the pack. Power–pulse was released in 1982.

COX

ROCKET LAUNCH SYSTEM

FOR LAUNCHING SOLID PROPELLANT MODEL ROCKETS

BATTERIES NOT INCLUDED. SEE CHART ON BACK PANEL.

LUNAR-LECTRIC LAUNCH SYSTEM

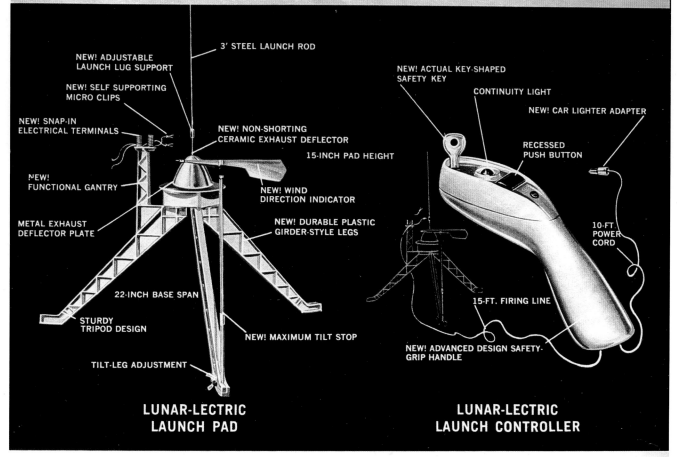

NEW! ADJUSTABLE LAUNCH LUG SUPPORT

3' STEEL LAUNCH ROD

NEW! SELF SUPPORTING MICRO CLIPS

NEW! SNAP-IN ELECTRICAL TERMINALS

NEW! NON-SHORTING CERAMIC EXHAUST DEFLECTOR

15-INCH PAD HEIGHT

NEW! FUNCTIONAL GANTRY

NEW! WIND DIRECTION INDICATOR

METAL EXHAUST DEFLECTOR PLATE

NEW! DURABLE PLASTIC GIRDER-STYLE LEGS

22-INCH BASE SPAN

STURDY TRIPOD DESIGN

NEW! MAXIMUM TILT STOP

TILT-LEG ADJUSTMENT

LUNAR-LECTRIC LAUNCH PAD

NEW! ACTUAL KEY-SHAPED SAFETY KEY

CONTINUITY LIGHT

NEW! CAR LIGHTER ADAPTER

RECESSED PUSH BUTTON

10-FT. POWER CORD

15-FT. FIRING LINE

NEW! ADVANCED DESIGN SAFETY-GRIP HANDLE

LUNAR-LECTRIC LAUNCH CONTROLLER

Now . . . the most professional launch pad ever! Loaded with new and exclusive features! Like a ceramic exhaust deflector to eliminate short-outs, tilt-leg adjustment to allow changes in flight direction, wind direction indicator to help calculate flight direction, adjustable launch lug support to allow use of all shapes of rockets, tripod design for maximum sturdiness, snap-in electrical terminals for easy use and positive wire hold. This is the launch pad rocketeers have been waiting for!

This is the launch controller that will make rocketeers forget everything they've seen before! For the first time . . . a launch controller with a car lighter adapter. It's the fast, easy way to set up a launching system . . . yet assures the presence of a responsible, safety-conscious rocketeer. And for the first time . . . a controller with a handle for sure-grip comfort and safety. And the push-button is recessed to assure deliberate launchings. This is the only controller rocketeers will be using!

STOCK NO.	ITEM		DOZ. PER CARTON	RETAIL PRICE
R-150	LAUNCH PAD		1	$5.00
R-151	LAUNCH CONTROLLER		1	$5.00
R-152	PAD & CONTROLLER		1	$9.50

Packed one dozen per shipping carton. Freight prepaid on $250.00 or more.
Orders less than $250.00 shipped collect.

MODEL PRODUCTS CORPORATION · MOUNT CLEMENS, MICHIGAN 48043

REFERENCES

Cadbury, Deborah. *Space Race: The Epic Battle between America and the Soviet Union for Dominion of Space*. New York: HarperCollins, 2006.

Estes Industries LLC. https://estesrockets.com/catalogs/.

Model Rockets. http://www.ninfinger.org/rockets/rockets.html.

NASA. NASA.gov.

National Association of Rocketry. NAR.org.

Sanford, Bob. "The Enerjet Story." *Launch Magazine*, November–December 2007. https://forums.rocketshoppe.com/attachment.php?attachmentid=63971.

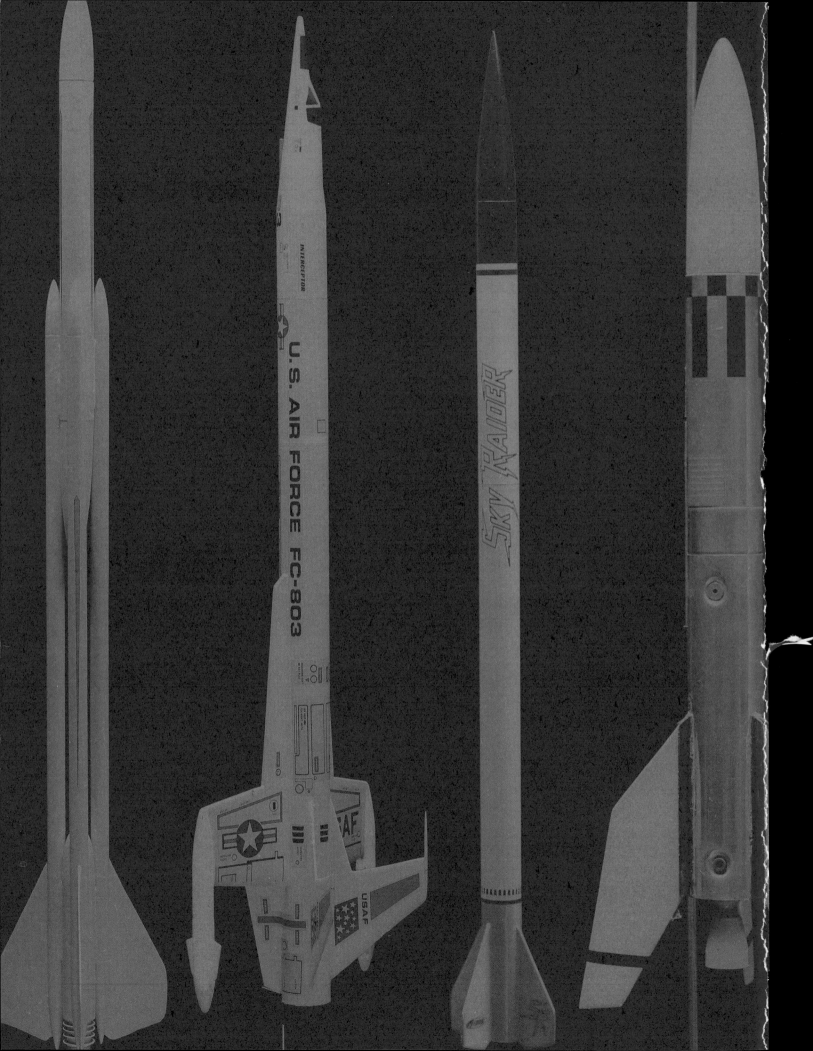